THE LA'
AMERIU...
REVOLUTION?

The 1994 Elections
and
Their Implications for Governance

THE LATEST AMERICAN REVOLUTION?

The 1994 Elections
and
Their Implications for Governance

Clyde Wilcox
Georgetown University

St. Martin's Press
New York

Executive editor: Don Reisman
Development: Susan Cottenden
Managing editor: Patricia Mansfield Phelan
Project editor: Talvi Laev
Art director: Lucy Krikorian
Text design: Dorothy Bungert/EriBen Graphics
Graphics: MacArt Design
Photo research: Rose Corbett Gordon
Cover design: Lucy Krikorian
Cover photo: David Scull/NYT Pictures

Library of Congress Catalog Card Number: 95-67060

Manufactured in the United States of America.

9 8 7 6 5
f e d c b

For information, write to:
St. Martin's Press, Inc.
175 Fifth Avenue
New York, NY 10010

ISBN: 0-312-13299-9

Foreword

"All politics is local."

TIP O'NEILL, *former Speaker of the House of Representatives*

Tip O'Neill's much-quoted aphorism is accurate for most midterm elections. Local personalities and issues usually dominate the campaign and explain the outcome from state to state. The elections of 1994 were different. They were the closest we have come to a national referendum in a midterm election since 1946. They were a vote of no confidence in Democratic leadership in general and the Clinton administration in particular. But they were more than that. They were also a protest against politics as usual, against the way that Congress worked and its members behaved, and against the policies and leadership in Washington and many of the states. The elections are already having a major impact on the politics of American government. That is why we refer to these elections as the latest American revolution.

The elections have affected the political landscape. The advantage that the Democrats obtained from their 1992 electoral victory has all but dissipated. Power has shifted in Washington and in many of the states. Not only have the Republicans gained control of both houses of Congress and more than half of the governorships, as well as achieving parity in the state legislatures, but they have seized the policy initiative. At least in the short run, it is the GOP that is determining the agenda, defining the issues, and setting the parameters of debate. And the public expects it to do so. A survey conducted by the Gallup organization in December of 1994 found that a plurality of Americans looked to the Republican leadership in Congress, not the president, to take the lead in solving the nation's problems.[1]

The fallout from the elections is not limited to national politics and policy. It extends to the entire federal system. By raising the issues of how much authority and responsibility the states should assume in designing and implementing social programs and who should pay for these programs, the elections have reopened a debate on federalism that is apt to influence federal-state relations for the foreseeable future.

The courts are also likely to become involved. Legislative enactments regarding term limits, balanced budgets, unfunded mandates, perhaps even prayer in schools are likely to end up as justiciable issues, some reaching the Supreme Court this term.

New and controversial policy questions, shifting political coalitions, and continued institutional rivalries, now reinforced by partisanship at the national level, are already generating significant political activity among interest groups. This activity, in turn, is bound to affect public opinion, which then influences the positions that the president and members of Congress take. What the government does and how it does it will also continue to shape the public mood, a mood that is hopeful of beneficial change yet doubtful of the government's ability to enact it.

And then there are the implications for the 1996 presidential election. With Republican chances improved, there are already a plethora of GOP candidates, potential Democratic challengers to the president, and the prospect of several independent presidential campaigns from candidates as diverse as Jesse Jackson and Ross Perot. The news media are having a field day covering the continuous campaign, partisan politics, and contentious policy debate.

Professor Clyde Wilcox skillfully addresses these developments which make up the politics of American government. He not only examines the results of the elections, but he dissects the vote and explains its meaning. He does not merely note personnel changes but discusses their impact on government processes, institutional interaction, and public policy. In this way he brings the politics of American government up to date and continues the saga of our democracy in action.

Stephen J. Wayne
Georgetown University

The Latest American Revolution? is offered for sale at a modest cost to your students. It is also available as a *free* supplement to adopters of *The Politics of American Government* by Stephen Wayne, Calvin Mackenzie, David O'Brien, and Richard Cole. For more information, please contact your local St. Martin's Press representative or call the St. Martin's Press college desk at 1-800-446-8923.

---

[1]"Public Expects GOP Miracles," *Times Mirror Center for the People and the Press*, December 8, 1994, p. 15.

Contents

INTRODUCTION

When the magnitude of Republican gains in the 1994 midterm elections became apparent, politicians and journalists scrambled to find a proper metaphor to describe the historic event. Many writers likened the election to a meteor strike or tidal wave because it had greatly altered the American political landscape.

Democrats had controlled the House of Representatives since 1952, enjoying by far the longest period of single-party control in United States history.[1] Indeed, the youngest members of the newly elected House had not yet been born when Republicans last enjoyed a majority in that chamber. Only one Democratic House member, Sidney Yates (D-Illinois), had ever served in a Republican-controlled House. (Yates is 88 years old and was first elected in 1950.) The 1994 elections ended this long-standing Democratic control. Republicans gained fifty-two seats in the House of Representatives to capture a majority for the first time in more than a generation. A number of influential Democratic incumbents lost their seats, including Speaker of the House Tom Foley, who became the first Speaker to lose a seat in more than 130 years, and House Ways and Means Committee Chair Dan Rostenkowski. Figure 1, a map of the House delegations in the 104th Congress (on p. 2), shows which party holds the majority in each state. The chart below the figure shows the net change in the Republican party's representation from the 103rd to the 104th Congress.

All Republican incumbents who sought reelection to the House, Senate, or a governorship won in 1994. Thirty-five Republican challengers beat House Democratic incumbents, three Republican challengers beat Democratic Senate incumbents, and five Republican gubernatorial challengers defeated Democratic incumbent governors. Republicans also won a disproportionate share of open governorships and seats in the House and Senate. Figure 2 (on p. 4) shows which party captured the governorship in each state.

The new Senate contains fifty-three Republicans and forty-seven Democrats. Eleven members are freshmen, including Olympia Snowe of Maine, who increases the number of women in the Senate to eight. Republicans now hold a 230 to 204 advantage in the House, with the one independent candidate expected to vote with Democrats on most issues. Republicans also control the governor's mansion in thirty states. They now hold the governorships in eight of the nine most populous states and also in a number of southern states, including Alabama, Texas, Oklahoma, and Tennessee. In addition, Republicans also made substantial gains in state legislatures, picking up fifteen state legislative chambers and tying three others. Figure 3 (on p. 6) shows which states elected Republicans to the Senate in 1994 and also shows the partisanship of senators from each state.

1

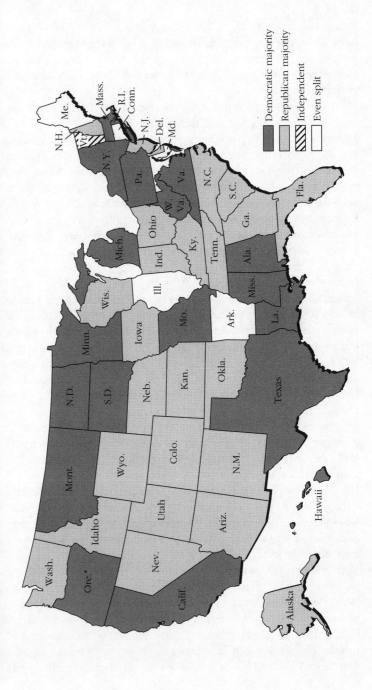

F I G U R E   1

House Delegations in the 104th Congress

Democratic majority
Republican majority
Independent
Even split

	Current Lineup	New Lineup	Net GOP Change		Current Lineup	New Lineup	Net GOP Change
Ala.	4D 3R	4D 3R	0	Mont.	1D 0R	1D 0R	0
Alaska	0D 1R	0D 1R	0	Neb.	1D 2R	0D 3R	+1
Ariz.	3D 3R	1D 5R	+2	Nev.	1D 1R	0D 2R	+1
Ark.	2D 2R	2D 2R	0	N.H.	1D 1R	0D 2R	+1
Calif.	30D 22R	27D 25R	+3	N.J.	7D 6R	5D 8R	+2
Colo.	2D 4R	2D 4R	0	N.M.	1D 2R	1D 2R	0
Conn.	3D 3R	3D 3R	0	N.Y.	18D 13R	17D 14R	+1
Del.	0D 1R	0D 1R	0	N.C.	8D 4R	4D 8R	+4
Fla.	10D 13R	8D 15R	+2	N.Dak.	1D 0R	1D 0R	0
Ga.	7D 4R	4D 7R	+3	Ohio	10D 9R	6D 13R	+4
Hawaii	2D 0R	2D 0R	0	Okla.	3D 3R	1D 5R	+2
Idaho	1D 1R	0D 2R	+1	Ore.	4D 1R	3D 2R	+1
Ill.	12D 8R	10D 10R	+2	Pa.	11D 10R	11D 10R	0
Ind.	7D 3R	4D 6R	+3	R.I.	1D 1R	2D 0R	-1
Iowa	1D 4R	0D 5R	+1	S.C.	3D 3R	2D 4R	+1
Kan.	2D 2R	0D 4R	+2	S.Dak.	1D 0R	1D 0R	0
Ky.	3D 3R	2D 4R	+1	Tenn.	6D 3R	4D 5R	+2
La.	4D 3R	4D 3R	0	Texas	21D 9R	19D 11R	+2
Maine	1D 1R	1D 1R	0	Utah	2D 1R	1D 2R	+1
Md.	4D 4R	4D 4R	0	Vt.	0D or 1I	0D or 1I	0
Mass.	8D 2R	8D 2R	0	Va.	7D 4R	6D 5R	+1
Mich.	10D 6R	9D 7R	+1	Wash.	8D 1R	2D 7R	+6
Minn.	6D 2R	6D 2R	0	W.Va.	3D 0R	3D 0R	0
Miss.	5D 0R	4D 1R	+1	Wis.	4D 5R	3D 6R	+1
Mo.	6D 3R	6D 3R	0	Wyo.	0D 1R	0D 1R	0

SOURCE: *Congressional Quarterly Weekly Report*, Nov. 12, 1994, p. 3236. Reprinted by permission.

3

FIGURE 2

Governors after the 1994 Election

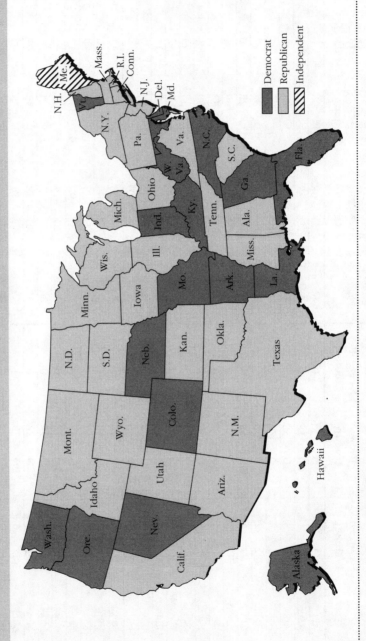

SOURCE: *Congressional Quarterly Weekly Report*, Nov. 12, 1994, p. 3249. Reprinted by permission.

4

Perhaps the most frequently used metaphor to describe these sweeping Republican victories was that of an earthquake. Although the 1994 election would clearly rate high on any political Richter scale, it is not yet clear whether it qualifies as the long-awaited "big one": the realignment of the electorate into a new Republican majority. Critical elections are best identified through hindsight, since they mark permanent changes in the balance of power between the parties. Democrats gained control of Congress in 1933 and maintained it for most of the next sixty years. In 1946, however, when Democrats lost fifty-five seats in the House, giving the Republicans control, and President Harry Truman's approval levels hit record lows, the results were not so long-lasting. Two years later the Democrats won back fifty-five seats and Truman won reelection. And, although Republicans controlled the Senate for the first six years of the Reagan administration, Democrats regained a majority in 1986. Whether the 1994 elections constitute a realignment will depend essentially on the longevity of the Republican majority.

Republicans called the 1994 elections a revolution and promised a corresponding revolution in policy. Republican leaders maintain that their prospects for keeping a majority will depend on their ability to produce legislation that appeals to voters. Newt Gingrich (R-Georgia), selected by House Republicans by acclamation to be Speaker of the House, vowed that the House would spend its first 100 days voting on the bills promised in the Republican "Contract with America." The Contract called for major reforms in legislation dealing with crime, welfare, taxes, and politics. Gingrich claimed that the elections gave Republicans a mandate to reinvent Congress and to trim or even eliminate many social programs that are part of what he calls the "corrupt welfare state."

Some Republicans went even further, arguing that the 1994 elections constituted a mandate to dismantle the welfare state and reverse four decades of liberal policies. Texas Senator Phil Gramm argued that the election was a mandate for conservative Republican policies, not those of his moderate Republican colleagues. Immediately after the election, Gramm stated of one such colleague that "[Senator] John Chafee's [R-Rhode Island] views were not endorsed by voters. . . . The views of the conservative majority within our caucus were endorsed." Chafee's moderate Republican views were endorsed by the voters of Rhode Island, at least, who returned him to the Senate with an overwhelming margin.

Elections carry multiple messages, and one aspect of the politics of elections concerns the struggle to define their meaning. To fully understand the meaning and implications of the 1994 elections, it is necessary to consider several questions. First, to what extent can we consider the 1994 elections a mandate for the programs Republicans hope to advance? Second, do the results signal a permanent realignment in American politics and the emergence of a Republican majority? Third, what are the implica-

FIGURE 3

The Senate in the 104th Congress

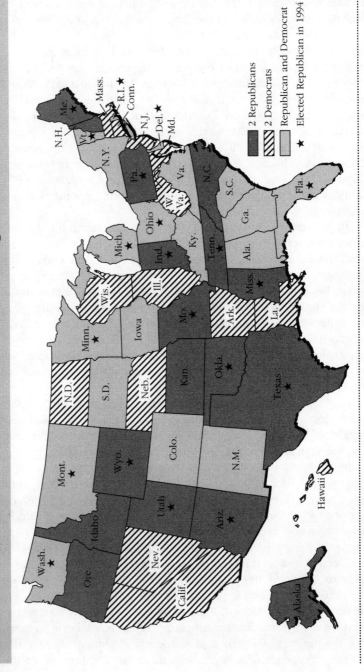

Legend:
- 2 Republicans
- 2 Democrats
- Republican and Democrat
- ★ Elected Republican in 1994

SOURCE: *Congressional Quarterly Weekly Report*, Nov. 12, 1994, p. 3246. Reprinted by permission.

tions of the elections for the way that Congress conducts itself? Finally, what are the likely political consequences for the interactions between the president and Congress, between House and Senate Republicans, and between Republicans and Democrats in the Congress?

WHO HAS THE MANDATE?

When Bill Clinton won the presidency in 1992, he triumphantly declared that the election was a mandate for renewed government action to better the lot of average Americans. The voters, he insisted, wanted national health care, job retraining, educational reform, and other liberal programs. Two years later, congressional Republicans claimed that their new majority constituted a mandate for a very different set of policies in health care, welfare, labor market economics, and education and for a radical reduction of the scope of government action.

It has become a tradition in American politics for winning candidates to claim that the election constituted a mandate for policies they advocated during the campaign, and for losing candidates and parties to offer more limited interpretations of the meaning of the election. The struggle to define the meaning of an election has political consequences, for political elites frequently act according to their interpretation of election returns. When Democrats interpreted Reagan's surprisingly large victory margin in 1980 as a mandate for cuts in taxes and domestic spending and a boost in defense spending, they provided the votes needed to pass much of Reagan's legislative program in his first year. When they interpreted his even larger 1984 victory margin as the triumph of personal popularity and a "Teflon" presidency, they were far less supportive of Reagan's agenda.

To determine whether the 1994 elections constituted a mandate for Republican policies, it is necessary to put the election into context. First, how did the Democratic losses in the 1994 midterm elections compare with previous midterm results and with political science theories? Second, how did Democratic incumbents fare in the elections? Third, do the patterns of vote choice tell us anything about the meaning of the 1994 elections? Finally, what can we learn from exit polls, referenda outcomes, and other data about the meaning of the 1994 elections?

Midterm Elections: Presidential Nightmares

It is not surprising that Democrats lost seats in the 1994 elections. Perhaps the single most common outcome of American electoral politics is that the party of the president loses seats in the midterm election. In all but one election since 1862, the president's party has lost seats in the House of Representatives at the midterm election, and in most of these elections it has lost Senate seats as well. In some elections these losses have been modest: in 1962 the Democrats lost only four seats, and in 1986 the Republicans lost just five. In other elections the losses have been far larger. In 1894, Grover Cleveland's Democratic party lost 116 seats, more than half of the seats they had held. The last substantial loss of seats occurred in 1974 in the aftermath of the Watergate scandal, when the Republicans lost forty-eight seats.

Figure 4 shows the number of House seats lost by the president's party in each midterm election since 1946. Five of these elections have resulted in major partisan shifts in seats—in 1946, in 1958, in 1966 in the midst of the Vietnam War, in 1974 after the Watergate investigations culminated in Nixon's resignation, and in 1994. The other eight elections resulted in more modest losses. Seen in this light, Democratic losses in 1994 are large but certainly not unprecedented.

Outcomes of Senate races are somewhat less predictable because only thirty-three or thirty-four seats are contested in any given election, so that random factors such as retirements and the partisan distribution of contested seats have more influence on the outcome. Nevertheless, in most midterm elections, the president's party loses seats in the Senate as well.

Voting as a Referendum on the President's Performance

Political scientists have offered different explanations for why the president's party sometimes loses many seats and sometimes only a few. Some scholars view the midterm election as a referendum on the president's performance in office. Voters who are unhappy with the president vote against

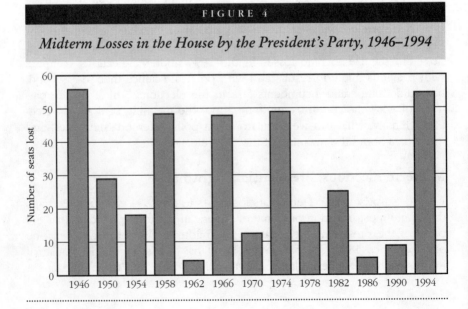

FIGURE 4

Midterm Losses in the House by the President's Party, 1946–1994

his party and those who are satisfied vote for candidates who share his partisanship. Presidents are generally less popular at the midterm than at the time of their election, for no president can meet the high expectations engendered by the presidential campaign and the "honeymoon" period that occurs immediately after he assumes office. Moreover, those voters who disapprove of the president's performance are more likely to vote in midterm elections than those who are satisfied. Scholars who adopt this view have developed elegant models that predict the losses by the president's party, basing these models primarily on economic indicators and presidential popularity.[2] When the economy is strong and the incumbent president is popular (as was the case with John Kennedy in 1962), the president's party generally loses only a few seats. When the economy is weak and the president unpopular (as with Richard Nixon in 1974), the losses are usually higher.

In autumn of 1994, the United States economy continued to exhibit significant growth with little inflation, but real disposable income had not risen over the past two years and a majority of Americans believed that the economy was still in recession.[3] Clinton's approval ratings were hovering slightly above 40 percent, nearly fifteen percentage points below the average presidential midterm approval levels, and in some segments of the population antipathy toward the president ran high. A poll by the Wirthlin Group found that although the public was evenly divided between those who approved and those who disapproved of Clinton's presidency, nearly twice as many Americans *strongly* disapproved as strongly approved. Thus part of the explanation for Democratic losses lies in public disapproval of Clinton and nervousness about the state of the economy. Still, statistical models that used economic indicators and measures of presidential popularity predicted that the Republicans would gain between five and twenty seats, far fewer than the actual increase.

The Quality of the Candidate Pool

Some political scientists point to the importance of decisions by potential candidates to help explain why the president's party sometimes loses many seats and sometimes loses just a few.[4] The quality and experience of the candidates recruited by each party vary across elections, and the party that recruits the best candidates has a clear advantage.

Skilled, experienced candidates are more likely than their opponents to win open seats, and they have the best chance of beating an incumbent. Experienced politicians generally bide their time, waiting for the best circumstances to launch a bid for higher office. The most viable candidates for the House of Representatives are those who hold state legislative, county, or city office, and the most viable candidates for the Senate are incumbent House members and those who hold statewide office. These individuals must almost always give up their current office to run for Congress, and so they usually wait until an incumbent retires or is weakened by scandal, or until national conditions favor their party. The collective decisions by potential candidates in each party shape the candidate pool and the eventual outcome of the election.

In 1994, the Republicans recruited a good set of House and Senate nonincumbent candidates, while the Democratic nonincumbent candidates were less experienced and skilled than in previous years.[5] Political scientist Gary Jacobson has noted that 1994 was one of only three elections since 1946 in which the Republicans' candidate pool was more experienced than the Democrats'.[6] Paul S. Herrnson, author of a recent book on congressional campaigns, noted that "in 1994, Republicans fielded an exceptional crop of challengers, many of whom raised or donated significant sums of money to their campaigns. These challengers waged highly sophisticated campaigns that relied on geodemographic techniques to target voters and used position issues, such as crime, gun control, and attacks on big government, to defeat their opponents."[7]

Part of the explanation for the Republicans' large gains, therefore, lies in the fact that they recruited more experienced and better-known candidates than did the Democrats. Yet statistical models that incorporate this relatively small differential in the quality of the candidate pool along with presidential popularity and the state of the economy predicted a Republican gain of twenty-five seats in the House, less than half of their actual gain. Herrnson concluded that "these models' failure to incorporate the quality of the campaigns the candidates waged is a major shortcoming."

Surge and Decline Theory

Finally, some political scientists suggest that the voting decisions of independents and the turnout of partisans help determine the magnitude of midterm losses. During a presidential election, turnout is higher among those who identify with the party of the winner. Moreover, independents disproportionately vote for the winning presidential candidate and for congressional candidates from the president's party. As a consequence, candidates from the president's party win in a number of close elections. In the following midterm election, the turnout advantage of the president's party will be negated or even reversed, and many independents will shift their vote. At least some of the newly elected members of the president's party will lose, producing a midterm loss.

At first glance, it might seem that this modified "surge and decline" theory would predict that the president's party must gain seats during a presidential year if they are to lose them in the midterm. However, the 1992 elections were one of a very few in American history in which the party of the winning presidential candidate actually *lost* seats, so it would appear that there was no surge from which to decline. Yet the modified surge and decline theory also applies to elections in which the president's party won more seats than it would normally be expected to win.

The 1992 presidential election was the first to be conducted after the 1990 redistricting, which created many new seats in Republican areas of the South and Southwest and reduced the number of seats in the predomi-

Wide World Photos

Thomas Foley, former Speaker of the House of Representatives, leaves public office to reenter private law practice. Foley lost the race in Washington's fifth district to newcomer George Nethercutt, ending a thirty-year congressional career.

nantly Democratic areas in and around northern cities. Many analysts had predicted big Republican gains in the House in 1992, but these failed to materialize in that election. In 1994, many of the Republicans' gains were in the geographic areas where they had expected to gain in 1992, and many of the Democratic incumbents who were defeated had been first elected in 1992 in these Republican areas. So an additional reason for Republican gains in 1994 was the delayed effect of the 1990 redistricting. Yet the modified surge and decline model that takes this redistricting into account predicted a net loss of approximately 18–22 seats.[8]

Overall, Democratic losses in the 1994 midterm election were larger than in most recent elections, in part because Clinton was unpopular, in part because the Republicans fielded better-known, more experienced candidates, and in part because the Republicans captured some seats that they might have won in 1992 but for George Bush's poor showing. However, Democratic losses were far larger than any of these traditional political science theories predicted. Most professional pollsters and politicians were also surprised by the magnitude of the gains. When asked why the Ohio GOP did better than even he had expected, one Ohio Republican leader said, "Sometimes the planets, the moon and the stars align just right, and one side wins more than they have any right to expect."[9]

The surprising magnitude of Republican gains has led some commentators to suggest that the voters have rejected the Democratic party, and that a new era of Republican dominance is at hand. Yet a look at incumbency reelection rates tells a somewhat different story.

Incumbents and Term Limits

The 1994 election resulted in the defeat of many prominent House and Senate incumbents. Tom Foley became the first Speaker of the House to lose his seat in more than a century. Many other House committee chairs lost, as did Senator Jim Sasser, the leading candidate to succeed retiring Senator George Mitchell as Democratic leader in the Senate. Yet, overall, more than 84 percent of House Democratic incumbents who sought reelection won, as did more than 87 percent of Democratic Senate candidates. It is likely that more Democrats would have lost but for the advantages of incumbency.

Incumbents win for a variety of reasons. They have enormous advantages in elections: they are better known, raise more money, and can usually command more free media attention. They can mail free materials to constituents throughout most of their terms, can travel free to their districts, and have large staffs to help them answer constituent mail and maintain other contacts. More than 90 percent of House incumbents who sought reelection in every election between 1968 and 1992 won, usually by comfortable margins. Senate incumbents have generally faced more formidable, better-funded opponents, but over the past two decades well

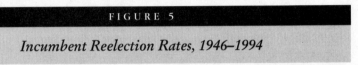

FIGURE 5

Incumbent Reelection Rates, 1946–1994

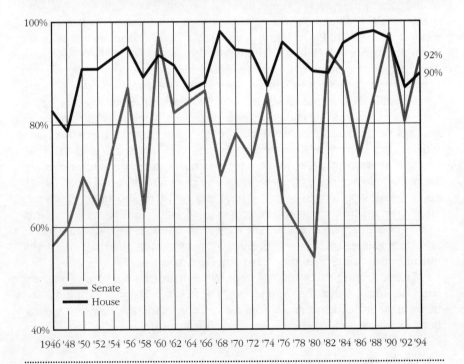

SOURCE: *Congressional Quarterly Weekly Report*, Nov. 12, 1994, p. 3237. Reprinted by permission.

KNOW WHAT I HATE ABOUT POLITICIANS?! — AS SOON AS THEY GET ELECTED, THEY TURN INTO INCUMBENTS!!

WASSERMAN
©'94 BOSTON GLOBE
DIST. BY L A TIMES SYND.

SOURCE: Copyright 1994, Boston Globe. Distributed by Los Angeles Times Syndicate. Reprinted by permission.

over 80 percent of those who sought reelection have won. Figure 5 shows the relative incumbent reelection rates in the House and Senate from 1946 through the present.

Yet incumbents do not win merely because they have electoral advantages. Most incumbents work hard to represent their state or district and are skilled candidates who have honed their campaign skills over the course of many elections. Over time, incumbents also come to know their constituents and their concerns.

Because incumbents usually win reelection, many Americans have called for limits on the number of terms that members can serve in the House and Senate. Not all states allow legislation through referenda, but of the twenty-four states that do permit this direct citizen lawmaking, twenty-two states have passed initiatives that limit the number of terms their incumbent Representatives and Senators can serve.

Despite the popularity of term limits referenda, a surprising number of voters in past elections have simultaneously voted for term limits and also voted to return their incumbent to office. In 1992 in Oregon, for example, more than half of all voters who supported term limits also voted to reelect a long-standing incumbent, Senator Bob Packwood. In part, this is because it is easy to imagine better candidates than the current incumbent but much harder to find those ideal citizens and persuade them to run. Presumably at least some voters hope that term limits will encourage more attractive candidates to run, yet prefer their incumbent to the opponent in that particular election.

The defeat of some very prominent Democrats such as Tom Foley and Dan Rostenkowski bolsters the argument of opponents of term limits, who note that voters can exercise term limits at any election they choose; if they don't like the incumbents, they can vote them out of office. However, the victory of a large majority of Democratic incumbents suggests that reports of the death of the Democratic party may be premature and that voting patterns in the 1994 election may have a subtler meaning than some commentators have suggested.

Voting in the 1994 Elections

Election outcomes are determined by two factors: who votes, and for whom they vote. Political professionals generally divide the potential electorate into demographic and ideological blocs that comprise the party coalitions, and then attempt to determine the turnout rate and vote choice of these groups. For example, Democratic candidates are usually helped by a high turnout among African Americans, while Republicans benefit from a high turnout among white evangelical Christians.

Republicans received more votes in the 1994 elections than they had in 1992 because their supporters voted at higher rates than Democratic constituency groups, and because some voting blocs supported Republican candidates in greater numbers than in past elections. Turnout among white evangelicals appears to have increased in 1994, while turnout among women and those younger than age 30 (two groups that tend to support Democratic candidates) was lower than in 1992.[10]

Table 1 shows the composition of the electorate in each election since 1984. The 1994 electorate was proportionately composed of more men and older citizens than were the electorates of 1990 and 1992. It was also somewhat more conservative and more Republican, probably in part because conservative Republicans were especially likely to vote and in part because more Americans identified themselves as conservative and Republican. The table shows only the percentage of the electorate who identified themselves as white Protestants, as Catholics, or as Jews, but one national exit poll showed that 23 percent of the 1994 electorate were white born-again Christians, while another showed that 5 percent were members of the Religious Right.[11]

The higher turnout among white evangelical Christians may have been due in part to concerted mobilization efforts by Christian Right groups such as the Christian Coalition, which distributed millions of voter's guides across the country. Some candidates visibly associated with the Christian Right lost in 1994—for example, Oliver North, who ran as a Republican in Virginia's Senate election—but candidates supported by the Christian Right also won in many states. Political scientist John Green noted that "in 1994 the Christian right expanded the sophistication and level of its grassroots effort to mobilize voters on behalf of Republican candidates. The Christian right appears to have helped a number of Republicans win close races in the South and the West, and thus contributed to the GOP's takeover of Congress and state governments."[12] Christian Coalition executive director

	1984	1986	1988	1990	1992	1994
SEX						
Male	49%	48%	48%	47%	46%	49%
Female	51%	52%	52%	53%	54%	51%
AGE						
18-29	23%	16%	20%	16%	22%	14%
30-59	53%	56%	58%	63%	62%	60%
60 +	22%	28%	22%	21%	16%	27%
RACE						
White	87%	86%	86%	91%	87%	85%
Black	9%	8%	9%	5%	8%	10%
Hispanic	2%	3%	3%	2%	3%	3%
PARTISANSHIP						
Democrat	38%	38%	35%	37%	39%	37%
Independent	26%	24%	25%	27%	28%	26%
Republican	35%	33%	35%	34%	34%	37%
RELIGION						
White Protestant	50%	45%	39%	47%	48%	46%
Catholic	26%	31%	27%	31%	27%	24%
Jewish	3%	4%	4%	4%	4%	3%
UNION MEMBER	14%	15%	13%	11%		
UNION HOUSEHOLD					19%	19%
IDEOLOGY						
Liberal	16%	16%	17%	19%	22%	18%
Moderate	44%	45%	45%	46%	50%	45%
Conservative	33%	32%	33%	34%	29%	37%

TABLE 1

The Composition of the Electorate, 1984–1994

Because of rounding, percentages may not add up to 100.

SOURCE: National exit polls from 1984 through 1992, as reported in the *National Journal*, Nov. 12, 1994.

Ralph Reed claimed that the extra evangelical turnout switched twenty-five House seats from Democrat to Republican.[13]

The Christian Right was not the only source of Republican mobilization. The National Rifle Association and other pro-gun groups, angered by

Wide World Photos

Talk radio was credited with an important role in determining voter turnout for the 1994 elections. Rush Limbaugh, shown here with former president George Bush, delivers his highly conservative political talk program to a claimed listenership of 20 million. Over half of the voters surveyed at the polls said that they listened to political talk radio shows some of the time, and 75 percent of the most frequent listeners voted for Republican candidates.

a 1994 ban on certain assault rifles, made a concerted effort to bring their supporters to the polls to vote out the (mainly Democratic) incumbents who had supported the ban. A national exit poll by Mitofsky International showed that 37 percent of 1994 voters considered themselves supporters of the NRA.

Advocates of term limits, who have built a grassroots movement of dedicated supporters, also mobilized on behalf of the Republicans who promised to pass term limits legislation. Talk radio shows may also have been a source of Republican mobilization. Although most scholars believe that these programs generally preach to the converted, the programs do increase the anger of conservative listeners. In 1994, radio talk show hosts accused Clinton of a variety of misdeeds, and some hinted openly that he may have been involved in murder. Even if these shows do not change votes, they may increase turnout of their listeners. One national exit poll showed that 21 percent of the electorate were frequent listeners of talk radio.

David Price, a political scientist who was defeated in a bid for reelection to the House in North Carolina in 1994, noted that he was "caught in a double movement of adverse national trends and an extraordinary local Republican mobilization that included conservative Christian groups, gun groups, anti-tax groups, and those who listen to the conservative talk radio shows that blanket eastern North Carolina."[14] This diverse mobilization resulted in a larger number of Republican voters.

Exit poll data reported in the *New York Times* suggest that some groups also changed their voting patterns in 1994. Republicans and conservatives were less likely to support Democratic incumbents than in previous elections, especially in the South. In past elections, Democratic incumbents had managed to win a significant number of votes from conservative Republicans by focusing their campaigns on local issues and on their ability to win congressional appropriations that benefited their district. Gary Jacobson noted after the election that in 1994, Republicans succeeded in nationalizing the congressional elections.[15] For once, Tip O'Neill's famous adage that "all politics is local" did not apply.

More importantly, independents favored Republican candidates in 1994, after nearly a decade of tilting toward the Democrats. Table 2 (on p. 18) shows that 10 percent more independents voted for Republican candidates in 1994 than in 1992, and the swing was even greater among independents who had voted for Ross Perot in 1992. Perot asked his supporters to vote Republican in 1994 to give that party a chance, and then to hold them accountable. Whether Perot's call produced the shift in independent voting, however, is not clear. Many of Perot's independent supporters in 1992 were conservatives and/or young white men and would have been expected to support Republican candidates in any event. Perot did endorse two Democrats, including Democratic Texas Governor Ann Richards, who lost a close race in Perot's home state to George W. Bush.

Reuters/Bettmann

Incumbent Ann Richards smiles as challenger George W. Bush makes a point during their televised debate. Despite her personal popularity, Richards lost a close race, continuing the string of one-term governors in Texas.

TABLE 2

Portrait of the Electorate: Who Voted for Whom in the House

		1988		1990		1992		1994	
		Bush beats Dukakis but Republicans lose two House seats.		Democrats gain amid fears of war and recession.		Clinton wins presidency, but has no coattails in the House.		For the first time in 40 years, the Republicans win control of both House and Senate	
		DEM.	REP.	DEM.	REP.	DEM.	REP.	DEM.	REP.
%	TOTAL Vote for House	54	46	52	48	54	46	50	50
49	Men	52	48	51	49	52	48	46	54
51	Women	57	43	54	46	55	45	54	46
79	Whites	50	50	50	50	50	50	42	58
13	Blacks	85	15	79	21	89	11	88	12
5	Hispanics	76	24	72	28	72	28	70	30
13	18–29 years old	54	46	52	48	55	45	54	46
35	30–44 years old	54	46	53	47	53	47	48	52
28	45–59 years old	54	46	51	49	52	48	51	49
25	60 and older	55	45	53	47	56	44	51	49
69	Married	52	48	52	48	50	50	46	54
31	Not married	54	46	59	41	61	39	54	46
5	Not a high school graduate	63	37	60	40	67	33	68	32
22	High school graduate	57	43	56	44	58	42	52	48
32	Some college	53	47	52	48	53	47	47	53
41	College graduate or more	50	50	51	49	50	50	49	51
22	College graduate	47	53	50	50	46	54	45	55
19	Post-graduate education	54	46	53	47	55	45	54	46
23	From the East	54	46	54	46	54	46	52	48
25	From the Midwest	55	45	49	51	46	54	44	56
30	From the South	54	46	54	46	49	51	45	55
22	From the West	53	47	54	46	49	51	59	41
41	White Protestant	44	56	45	55	43	57	34	66
29	Catholic	55	45	54	46	57	43	52	48
4	Jewish	68	32	73	27	79	21	78	22
20	White born-again Christian	34	66	34	66	34	66	24	76

TABLE 2 (cont'd)

Portrait of the Electorate: Who Voted for Whom in the House

		1988		1990		1992		1994	
		DEM.	REP.	DEM.	REP.	DEM.	REP.	DEM.	REP.
11	Family income under $15,000	67	33	63	37	69	31	62	38
20	$15,000 to $29,999	57	43	55	45	57	43	52	48
30	30,000 to $49,999	53	57	52	48	52	48	49	51
39	Over $50,000	45	55	49	51	47	53	46	54
17	Over $75,000	—	—	—	—	44	56	47	53
8	Over $100,000	39	61	43	57	—	—	45	55
	Standard of living is:								
21	Getting better	—	—	51	49	34	66	66	34
23	Getting worse	—	—	54	46	72	28	37	63
55	Staying the same	—	—	54	46	50	50	50	50
35	Republicans	21	79	23	77	15	85	7	93
24	Independents	54	46	52	48	54	46	44	56
41	Democrats	83	17	79	21	89	11	90	10
18	Liberals	80	20	73	27	81	19	82	18
48	Moderates	57	43	56	44	57	43	58	42
34	Conservatives	34	66	37	63	28	72	21	79
25	Union household	63	37	—	—	67	33	63	37
55	Employed	52	48	51	49	51	49	48	52
40	White men	47	53	48	52	49	51	38	62
40	White women	52	48	52	48	51	49	45	55
6	Black men	82	18	79	21	84	16	85	15
7	Black women	88	12	80	20	92	8	90	10

1994 data were collected by Mitofsky International based on questionnaires completed by 5,260 voters leaving polling places around the country on election day. 1990 and 1992 data were collected by Voter Research and Surveys based on questionnaires completed by 15,490 voters in 1992 and 19,888 voters in 1990. Data for 1988 were based on surveys of 11,645 voters conducted by the *New York Times* and CBS News. Dashes indicate that a question was not asked or a category was not provided in a particular year. Those who gave no answer are not shown. Family income categories in 1988: Under $12,500, $12,500–$24,999, $25,000–$34,999, $35,000–$49,999, $50,000–$100,000, and over $100,000. In 1990: Under $15,000, $15,000–$29,999, $30,000–$49,999, $50,000–$99,999, and $100,000 or over. In 1992: Under $15,000, $15,000–$29,999, $30,000–$49,999, $50,000–$74,999, and $75,000 or over. In 1994: Under $15,000, $15,000–$29,999, $30,000–$49,999, $50,000–$74,999, $75,000–$99,999, and $100,000 or over. Born-again Christian was labeled "Born-again/Evangelical Christian" in 1994, "Born-again Christian/Fundamentalist" in 1992, "Fundamentalist or evangelical Christian" in 1988 and 1990. The question about standard of living in 1990 was "Compared to 2 years ago, is your family's financial situation better today, worse today or about the same?" In 1994 the question was "Compared to 4 years ago, is your family's financial situation better today, worse today or about the same?" Men and women college graduates include those with post-graduate education.

SOURCE: *New York Times*, Nov. 13, 1994. Copyright ©1994 by The New York Times Company. Reprinted by permission.

The shift to Republicans was confined to white voters and was some-what greater in the South and Midwest, although it occurred in all regions of the country. It was also primarily confined to men, creating a larger gender gap than had been evident in previous elections. Men preferred Republican candidates by 55 to 45 percent, while women favored Democratic candidates by the same margin. Yet men turned out in greater numbers than in past elections, so this growing gender gap benefited Republicans. A full 62 percent of white men voted for Republican candidates in 1994. Democratic pollster Celinda Lake maintained that white male voters were especially frustrated with Clinton. "They thought this country boy from Arkansas who ate at McDonald's was someone they could talk to, and he forgot about them. And they pay back those who forget them."[16]

Republicans benefited from an electoral mobilization of key conservative groups and from a change in the voting patterns of whites and of men who were Republicans or independents. These factors led to a small aggregate shift in total votes that produced a large change in the composition of Congress.

Is 1994 a Mandate for Republican Policies?

Many political scientists are skeptical of claims that elections constitute mandates for at least three reasons.[17] First, important national elections frequently do not produce a clear-cut winner. Although Clinton claimed a mandate in 1992, he received only 43 percent of the popular vote, suggesting that the public was not uniformly behind his policies. Exit polls in 1994 indicated that the Republicans received slightly more than 50 percent of votes cast in the House elections. The exit poll data presented in the *New York Times* show that since 1984, Republicans have received between 46 and 49 percent of the popular vote in House elections, so the 1994 totals indicate a net shift of between 1 and 4 percent. A narrow victory resulting from a small shift in aggregate voting does not constitute a call to dismantle the welfare state.

How can such a small shift in voting produce such a large net change in seats? The answer lies in the design of the American electoral system. Many European nations apportion their legislatures according to the proportion of votes awarded to each party. Under such a system, the Democrats and Republicans would have had almost equal strength for more than a decade. The United States apportions the Senate and House on a winner-takes-all basis. In every country with such a system, the winning party almost always gains more seats than it would have captured in a proportional system.

To see why this is so, imagine that each Republican candidate for the House wins the election with 50.1 percent of the popular vote. In a proportional representation system, the Republicans would have a tiny major-

MIRANDA WARNING

1. You have the right to remain silent.
2. Anything you say can and will be used against you in a court of law.
3. You have the right to talk to a lawyer and have him present with you while you are being questioned.
4. If you cannot afford to hire a lawyer, one will be appointed to represent you at county expense before any questioning, if you wish.
5. If you give up your right to remain silent, and later wish to stop answering questions, no further questions will be asked.

WAIVER

1. Do you understand each of these rights I have explained to you?
2. Having these rights in mind, do you wish to talk to me now?

SIGNATURE

OFFICER ADVISING RIGHTS

Time

Date

Jnited States, they would hold every seat, / election. Throughout the 1980s, Demo-)f House seats than their share of House true for Republicans.)olicy mandate was made stronger by their .ppendix A), which was signed by more d candidates and published in *TV Guide*. le opportunity to acquaint itself with the al scientists are skeptical of mandates for a :nerally found that House elections, and to s as well, do not hinge on policy issues. their incumbents beyond recognizing their en recognize the name of the challenger.)eared to be aware that Democrats had con- atives for forty years. Soon after the election ition to the new Republican House majority, ved that nearly 20 percent of respondents ntrolled the new House of Representatives, ;. It is likely that many fewer knew which *fore* the election. When voters were asked in 1900 ... le House of Representatives, 29 percent were unwilling to hazard a guess. An additional 12 percent guessed that the Republicans held a majority. If we correct for guessing, fewer than half of the survey respondents knew that Democrats controlled the House.[18] In one 1990 survey, fewer than one in three respondents correctly identified the Republican party as more conservative than the Democrats.[19]

Although the Republicans publicized their "Contract with America" widely, one *Los Angeles Times* poll conducted before the election showed that fewer than 20 percent of the public had heard of the program and only one in four of those who planned to vote for Republican candidates knew anything about the Contract. Moreover, of those who had heard of the Contract, more than half termed it "unrealistic." A report by the Wirthlin group found that only 4 percent of voters surveyed before the election had heard of the Contract and approved it. Pollsters for both Republican and Democratic candidates reported that Democratic candidates gained ground after the Contract was announced, suggesting that ultimately some voters supported Republican candidates *in spite of* the Contract, not because of it. Clearly, the election cannot constitute a mandate for the Contract.

A final reason why political scientists are skeptical of mandates is that the vote is an exceptionally blunt instrument for sending messages to elected officials. In any given race, the candidates take many different positions on issues, and most voters find themselves attracted by some stands of both candidates. Winning candidates usually claim an endorsement for all of their policy positions, although voters may have supported them primarily because of a single issue.

The Meaning of the Vote

Although votes for candidates may have multiple meanings, we can get a somewhat clearer view of the meaning of the vote by examining the outcomes of statewide referenda. In many states, voters in 1994 considered ballot initiatives that would become law if a majority of voters approved. As in previous years, the political content of referenda passed in various states suggests that the voters were not endorsing a single ideological position.

Term limits passed in seven of the eight states that voted on them in 1994, bringing to twenty-two the number of states that have enacted such limits.[20] Missouri, Montana, Oregon, and Nevada passed stricter campaign finance laws, whereas voters in Colorado and Massachusetts defeated such measures. Voters in Nevada passed a bill requiring a super majority in the state legislature to approve of new taxes, but voters in Missouri, Montana, and Oregon all rejected such a requirement.

A measure that would have created criminal penalties for doctors who performed abortions except in cases of rape, incest, or risk to the woman's life failed in Wyoming, as did referenda in two states that would have limited the protections extended to gay men and lesbians. Oregon made it legal for terminally ill patients to obtain prescriptions for lethal drugs, thereby effectively allowing suicide. Oregon also voted to ban the hunting of black bears with bait and that of cougars with dogs. Washington made it illegal for anyone but a dentist to make and sell false teeth, and Alaska decided not to move its state capital to Wasilla.

Perhaps the most controversial referendum was California's Proposition 187, which bans the use of state monies to provide any social services except emergency medical care to illegal immigrants and their children. The issue became a key component of Governor Pete Wilson's (R-California) reelection campaign and divided the Republican party nationally. Presidential aspirants Jack Kemp and William Bennett both announced their opposition to the measure, which passed by a sizable margin.

Taken together, these referenda do not constitute a strong conservative mandate. Term limits continue to be popular, yet Republican proposals to make it more difficult for legislatures to raise taxes were rejected by voters in many states. Moreover, the social agenda of many conservative Republicans to limit abortions and civil rights for gay men and lesbians was rejected by voters. The immigration referendum in California cut across ideological lines, with strong conservatives such as Jack Kemp in opposition to it and other conservatives such as Patrick Buchanan giving it strong support.

In addition to examination of statewide referenda, a second way to determine the meaning of the vote is to ask voters directly what issues and factors determined their vote. To interpret the meaning of votes, pollsters ask voters as they exit the polls why they voted as they did, and both parties conduct extensive pre- and post-election focus groups and surveys. In

Reuters/Bettmann

Protesting the passage of Proposition 187 in California, hundreds of Latino stu-
dents demonstrate in downtown San Francisco in 1994. The constitutionality of
this referendum, which denies the use of state monies to provide social services to
illegal immigrants and their children, is being challenged in court.

1994, these polls and focus groups showed an angry and somewhat con-
fused electorate. Despite the robust economic growth, 55 percent of voters
surveyed in the Mitofsky International exit poll indicated that the country
was "off on the wrong track."

Although many House Democrats sought to place the blame for their
party's losses on the president, the exit polls suggested a different story. A
majority of voters indicated that their vote had nothing to do with Clinton,
27 percent indicated that they cast a vote to oppose Clinton, and 18 percent reported that their House vote was cast to support Clinton.[21] No single issue dominated the election. An exit poll by Voter News Service asked
voters which issue mattered most in deciding how they voted. Health care
was the most salient issue, selected by 30 percent of voters, most of whom
voted for Democratic candidates. Crime was the second most frequently
mentioned issue (25 percent), and voters who selected it split their votes
evenly between the parties. The economy and jobs ranked third (22 percent), and a majority of voters who selected this issue voted for Democratic candidates. Those voters who indicated their concern with the budget
deficit (17 percent), Clinton's performance (17 percent), taxes (18 percent),
or the need for change (15 percent) all tended to vote for Republican candidates.

One consistent theme that emerges from these studies is a dislike of big government, which manifests itself in two ways. First, the public is generally dissatisfied with the way government works. Second, it wants to reduce the size of government, primarily through cuts in spending.

There was ample evidence in polling data that the public is unhappy with government. Democratic pollster Fred Hartwig noted that voters in November signaled that government no longer passed the "smell test" and that they no longer trusted government. Republican pollster Frank Luntz, whose focus groups helped design the Republican "Contract with America," reported that these were the most frustrated, cynical, and angry voters he had ever encountered. This unfocused anger has been building for several consecutive election cycles, as evidenced by the growing number of states that have passed term limits referenda.

In addition, the public told pollsters that government was too big and powerful. Republican pollster Ed Goeas found that 78 percent of voters thought government was too intrusive, and Luntz found that 79 percent thought that the federal government was too powerful. A report by the Wirthlin Group found that 71 percent agreed that "government is not the answer—government is the problem," and half indicated that they would like to see the power of the federal government reduced. Hartwig noted that even in Alaska, where voters pay no state taxes of any kind, "controlling state spending" was the second most important issue for voters. Republicans quickly seized on these data to argue that the election constituted a mandate for cutting government spending.

Yet Democratic pollsters report that the public sent some conflicting signals on cuts in government spending. Stan Greenberg found that although 60 percent of voters wanted to cut government spending, 62 per-

Wide World Photos

Richard Gephardt (D-Missouri), newly elected House minority leader, now assumes the leadership of House Democrats. Gephardt quickly scooped President Clinton on his proposal for a tax cut and vowed to outdo the Republicans' "Contract with America" by delivering his own "more positive" plan designed to benefit middle-class double-income families.

cent wanted to protect Social Security and Medicare from budget cuts. Hartwig noted that despite the enthusiasm for cutting state spending in Alaska, his polls found no majority for cutting any single big-ticket item in the state budget. This finding is consistent with surveys from at least the last decade, in which the public has supported cutting government in the abstract but, when asked concrete questions about specific programs, has favored additional spending in many areas.

The 1994 elections therefore appear to signify that voters wanted change in the way government operates and a reduction in the size and intrusiveness of government. Republicans hope to use this opportunity to sharply cut the size and scope of government and will attempt to argue that they have a mandate to do so. Democrats will counter that the election was at best a call for political change, not for a total reversal of four decades of social policies. The truly national scope of Republican victories, and the fact that no Republican incumbent lost a seat in either the Senate or House or a governorship, provided the Republicans with an important advantage in the struggle to define the meaning of the 1994 elections.

In late 1994, Democrats appeared ready to concede that the election did mean a call for less government. The Clinton administration floated calls for the elimination of Cabinet agencies, and Clinton proposed a middle-class tax cut in an effort to counter Republican proposals. Richard Gephardt (D-Missouri) announced his own tax-cut plan two days before the president announced his proposal in a nationwide television address, both scooping the president and making it even more likely that such a proposal will pass in 1995.

AT LAST, THE REALIGNMENT?

At several points in American electoral history, one party has replaced another as the majority party. These realignments are sometimes described as "critical elections," although the process usually unfolds over two or three election cycles. Realignments can be recognized only in hindsight, for one of their defining characteristics is duration.

Past realignments have generally occurred at times of economic, social, and political upheaval such as the Civil War, the Industrial Revolution, and the Great Depression. Some political scientists have noted that these three realignments all occurred approximately thirty-six to forty years apart, suggesting some kind of regular cycle. If such a cycle exists, then the Republicans should have emerged as a majority party between 1972 and 1976. The Watergate scandal in the middle of this period produced a short-term swing toward the Democrats, however, and resulted in the 1976 election of Democratic president Jimmy Carter and many new House Democrats.

Since 1976, many political scientists and most Republicans have been waiting for signs of the emergence of a new Republican majority. Those who expected another realignment pointed to the increased polarization of the parties, the growing number of independent voters, and the numerous defections of southern Democratic officeholders to the Republican party as evidence that one was in the making.

The South and the Republican Party

Much of the speculation on realignment has focused on the South. Once solidly Democratic, southern states have supported Republican presidential candidates by large margins in most recent presidential elections. The only Democratic presidential candidates to win since 1968, Jimmy Carter and Clinton, were southerners, and they both lost the southern white vote. During the 1980s, Republicans made inroads into southern congressional delegations, won a number of governorships, and made significant gains in state legislatures.

The gradual Republican growth in state legislatures helped Republicans build the "farm team" that would run for Congress in 1994. During much of the 1980s, Republicans did not even field candidates in some southern districts, but by 1994 they had a set of candidates ready to make their run. Political scientist James E. Campbell notes that 1994 was the first year in which more Republicans than Democrats ran unopposed.

In 1994, Republicans finally captured a majority of House seats from southern states, and gained a narrow majority of Senate seats as well. Eight southern Democratic incumbents lost, and eleven more seats fell to the Republicans after a Democratic incumbent retired or lost in a primary. Many of these seats are likely to remain in Republican hands for some time, and some Democrats who won in conservative southern districts may face additional serious, well-funded Republican challengers in 1996. Nearly a quarter of Democrats in southern seats won with less than 55 percent of the vote, and they will be especially vulnerable in the next election. One southern Democratic senator, Richard Shelby of Alabama, changed parties immediately after the election to join the new Republican majority in the Senate. Democratic conservatives in the House, however, have so far refused to follow suit, preferring instead to try to push their party toward a more centrist course.

In 1994, Republicans also gained seats in state legislatures and local offices throughout the South. In North Carolina, for example, Republicans captured the House, winning sixty-seven seats in a body that had contained only six Republicans in 1976. Republicans also came within three votes of winning control of the North Carolina Senate, and within six votes of controlling a majority of county commissions. These unprecedented gains suggest that Republicans in the South now have a set of skilled politicians from which to recruit candidates to run for state and national office. Moreover, their majority status should make it easier to recruit Republicans to seek House seats.[22]

More than a third of southern Democratic seats are in special minority districts, and are likely to remain safely Democratic. It was the creation of these districts that helped Republicans make significant gains in 1994, for isolating black votes into specially contained, minority districts created more predominantly white, suburban districts that favored the Republicans. One observer estimated that the racial districting that created eight new black seats in Alabama, Georgia, Florida, and North Carolina also led to the creation of fifteen seats that were won by Republicans.[23] There are significant legal challenges to some of these districts, however, and the Supreme Court may yet hold that the creation of these districts is unconstitutional.

Even if the Republicans hold onto most of the new southern seats, however, that does not mean that they will necessarily maintain control of the House and Senate for a substantial period of time. Relatively small shifts in the aggregate House vote can produce substantial shifts in seats, and Democrats can regain control by winning only a dozen seats. They can also recapture the Senate if they tie the Republicans by gaining only three seats and Clinton wins reelection. In this case, Vice President Al Gore would cast the tie-breaking vote. If the Republicans win the presidency in 1996, the Democrats will need to win four Senate seats.

Clinton's Chances of Reelection

In late November of 1994, many political analysts had already written off Bill Clinton, and seemed convinced that the Republicans had a lock on the presidency in 1996. Polls showed that nearly two-thirds of Democrats wanted another candidate to challenge Clinton from within his party in the 1996 primaries. Presidents generally survive intra-party challengers in modern times; indeed, no president since Chester Arthur in 1884 has lost a primary to a challenger within his party. Yet such intra-party battles inevitably lead to defeat in the general election. Since 1972, three of four incumbent presidents—Ford, Carter, and Bush—faced intra-party challengers, and they each lost the general election. Republican leaders are outwardly confident that they will soon control both the presidency and the Congress.

Clinton may lose in 1996, but history suggests that presidential popularity at the midterm is no sure gauge of voting two years later. Two other presidents have had approval ratings in the same range as Clinton at their midterm—Reagan and Truman. Both won reelection. In 1990, President Bush was more popular than any president since pollsters began asking the public their views on presidential performance. He lost two years later, receiving just 38 percent of the popular vote.

Even if the Republicans were to win the White House and retain control of the Congress, however, that would not be definitive evidence of a realignment. Realignments are also marked by a change in the aggregate partisanship of voters. In 1994, most surveys showed that Democrats outnumbered Republicans in the general public by a small margin, and they have constituted a plurality of voters in almost every survey since the New Deal. The size of the Democratic advantage has waxed and waned—at one point during the Reagan administration Republicans pulled even with Democrats, but the Iran-contra revelations gave the Democrats another advantage. If 1994 was the start of a realignment, then more Americans will identify themselves as Republicans than as Democrats.

Many political scientists believe that the 1994 elections may be the critical election that signals the long-awaited realignment. A. James Reichley argues that "this could be a very big election, not just for Republicans but for the whole political system. This could be the signal of a realignment."[24] If so, it would signal a new era of Republican dominance of national government, and Republican majorities in the electorate. Richard Wirthlin, a leading Republican pollster, suggested that the election might constitute the last stage of the "rolling realignment," and one Wirthlin Group report after the election did report that Republicans outnumbered Democrats.

It is likely that Republican candidates will benefit from a substantial shift in the contribution behavior of corporate political action committees (PACs). Since 1982, corporate PACs have given a majority of their funds to

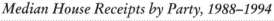

Financing the 1994 Elections

As the possibility of a Republican takeover of the House and Senate became evident, business groups and other conservatives increased their contributions to Republican nonincumbent candidates. As the figure below shows, the median House Republican challenger raised $145,000 in 1994, compared with $24,500 in 1990. More than a quarter of House Republican challengers raised at least $400,000—a figure that has historically indicated a significant possibility of victory.

Median House Receipts by Party, 1988–1994

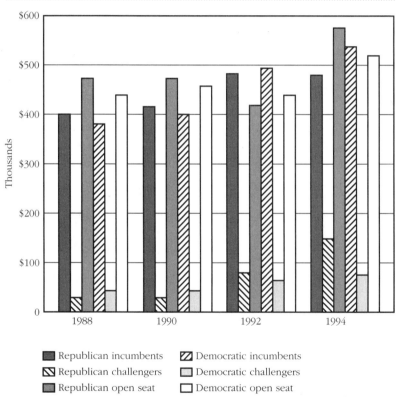

House Republicans challengers benefited from increased individual contributions and corporate PAC gifts. They also received substantial amounts from the campaigns of incumbent House members, who coordinated their efforts to share their receipts with candidates who needed it more. They relied slightly less on financing their own campaigns than House Republican challengers had in 1992.

In the Senate, two Republicans broke previous spending records, and both lost. Michael Huffington spent nearly $30 million (including nearly $28 million of his own money) in his quest to unseat Dianne Feinstein, and Oliver North raised almost $20 million, primarily in small donations solicited through the mail, in his losing race against Chuck Robb. That both men lost is additional proof that money by itself does not buy elections. Moreover, some candidates won while spending relatively small amounts. Michael Flanagan, who defeated Dan Rostenkowski in Illinois, spent only $107,000, compared to Rostenkowski's $2.3 million.[25]

Although spending substantial sums may not be sufficient or even necessary for victory, there is little doubt that money helps candidates win. Cash is especially useful to nonincumbent candidates, who must establish name recognition, and to incumbents early in their careers, before they have solidified their electoral base. In past elections, Democratic incumbents have raised substantial sums from corporate PACs and in individual contributions from corporate executives. This corporate money went to Democrats primarily because they controlled the House and Senate, and wrote the tax laws and other legislation that affected corporate profits. These corporate monies freed up labor PACs to contribute to Democratic nonincumbent candidates.

Most analysts expect that corporate money will now flow largely to Republican candidates. This happened when Republicans gained control of the Senate in the 1980 election. In that election, corporate PACs gave $8.35 million to Democratic candidates, and $8.98 million to Republicans. In 1982, the ratio shifted to $2.45 million for Democrats and $6.15 million for Republicans. In 1986, the election in which Democrats regained control, corporate PACs poured $14.4 million into the coffers of Republican candidates, compared with $4.8 million to Democrats. It is likely that corporate PACs and executives will make a similar shift in their contribution strategies in 1996.

Democratic incumbents who controlled House and later Senate committees. PAC officials described this behavior as "pragmatic," and admitted that they preferred Republican candidates but believed that it was necessary to give to Democrats to do business on Capitol Hill.[26] As the possibility of a Republican majority became evident in the fall of 1994, corporate and other conservative contributors opened their purses to pour record amounts into Republican candidate coffers. The new Republican incumbents should receive sizable contributions from corporate interests when they seek reelection.

... Or Perhaps Dealignment?

While some political scientists have waited for the realignment, others have argued that parties are becoming increasingly peripheral to the organization of politics and elections. One exit poll showed that 31 percent of voters were "fed up" with both political parties, and another post-election poll found that although most Americans were pleased with the Republican victory, they were also cynical that the Republicans would behave differently than the Democrats. Indeed, a majority of voters surveyed after the election indicated that they thought the new Republican majority would practice "politics as usual." Throughout the campaign, most pollsters and focus group directors described the electorate as more cynical than in any previous election. Some observers attributed this to the constant barrage of negative ads run by candidates of both parties.

The 1994 campaign was ideological, intense, and fiercely negative. Bill Carrick, consultant for Senator Dianne Feinstein of California, described the experience as "being in a mudbath for six months."[27] Curtis Gans, director of the Committee for the Study of the American Electorate, argued that such negative advertising undermined "the basic comity that's necessary for the functioning of the system, destroying respect for the process." One advertising firm ran an ad in the *Indianapolis Star* with a picture of two candidates strangling each other from out of televisions, and the caption "You know those political commercials you've been enjoying the past few months? We didn't do any of them."[28]

One reason that the public and some commentators may have perceived that the 1994 campaigns were especially negative was the limited range of issues debated in the election. Leonard Williams, an expert on advertising in Senate campaigns, noted that "the candidates had to score points within a relatively small degree of freedom: who is tougher on crime when we are all tough, who has raised or cut taxes when both candidates want their records to show cuts not raises, who is not telling the truth even though we know that politicians speak with forked tongues; who is or is not a politician, even though the act of seeking office should automatically define both candidates as one."[29]

An embattled Ted Kennedy (D-Massachusetts) aired the first negative ad of his thirty-two-year career in September and continued to attack his opponent throughout the campaign. The Senate race in Virginia was especially negative, with Oliver North and Charles Robb each attacking the other's personal character. One North ad featured the cover of a *Playboy* magazine with a headline reading "Tai Collins. The Woman that Senator

Virginia's Dirty Race

Wide World Photos

Although he outspent Chuck Robb by nearly 5 to 1, Oliver North lost a close election race in which 42 percent of the voters polled felt that neither candidate had the honesty or integrity needed to serve in the Senate.

When Charles (Chuck) Robb (D-Virginia) entered the U.S. Senate in 1988, his future seemed bright. After serving a successful term as governor of Virginia, he won an easy victory against token opposition. As a moderate, pragmatic southern Democrat, he was well positioned for an eventual run for the presidency, and his ties with others who shared his political views made it likely that he would be a major player in the Senate.

However, by spring of 1994, when Robb launched his reelection campaign, his star had dimmed substantially. He had spent much of the last six years defending himself against charges of personal misconduct. For years Virginia newspapers had carried stories of investigations into alleged misconduct, centering on charges that while governor he had attended parties where illegal drugs were used. Robb also narrowly escaped indictment on charges relating to the illegal taping of a cellular phone conversation of his longtime Democratic rival Douglas Wilder.

Tai Collins, a former Miss Virginia, did further damage to Robb's image by revealing details of an alleged affair with Robb in the pages of *Playboy* magazine, illustrated with nude photos of Collins. Robb denied the affair, but did admit to having spent time unclothed in Collins's hotel room drinking champagne. Robb insisted at the time that the only physical contact was a backrub. In spring of 1994, however, Robb issued a letter to Democratic activists admitting to extramarital sexual contact, but emphasizing that the contact had never included intercourse. Virginia's morally conservative voters were unimpressed by these nuanced distinctions.

In June of 1994, more than 14,000 Republicans converged on Richmond to select the candidate who would oppose Robb. The delegates selected Oliver North, the Marine officer in the Reagan White House whose testimony before the congressional Iran-contra hearings had electrified many on the political right. North was later convicted of perjury and many prominent Republicans questioned his honesty, although his conviction was overturned on a technicality. Ronald Reagan himself circulated a letter before the nomination in which he stated that he was getting "pretty steamed up" by North's accounts of Iran-contra. But North was nominated with the active support of Christian social conservatives mobilized by the Christian Coalition, and gun enthusiasts mobilized by the NRA and other groups.

Moderates in the party were outraged by North's selection. Mark Rozell, a specialist in Virginia politics, stated that the "Republicans have nominated the one person in Virginia who cannot beat Chuck Robb." Incumbent Senator John Warner refused to back North, and instead persuaded former Republican state attorney general Marshall Coleman to run as an independent. Former Democratic governor Douglas Wilder, Robb's longtime rival, also announced that he would run as an independent, setting up a four-candidate race. Wilder, the state's first African American governor, initially drew a good deal of African American support away from Robb.

Although Wilder's performance in debates drew widespread praise, a string of Robb endorsements by prominent black politicians and ministers led Wilder to withdraw from the race. After a private meeting with President Clinton, Wilder agreed to endorse Robb and to campaign for him in black churches across the state.

Both Robb and North were disliked by voters, and Coleman, the one independent left in the race, was personally well liked. On election day, however, many of his supporters decided not to waste their vote on a candidate who would surely lose, and instead voted for Robb. North led in the polls until the final weeks, but his momentum was stopped by a highly publicized speech in New York by Nancy Reagan, where she openly questioned North's honesty. Although North benefited from a coordinated voter mobilization drive by the Christian Right and gun groups, the mobilization against North by moderate Republicans and independents was larger.

Charles Robb Couldn't Resist." The announcer said, "Why can't Chuck Robb tell the truth? About the cocaine parties, where Robb said he never saw drugs. Then four of his party friends were sent to prison, for dealing cocaine. Or about the beauty queen in the hotel room in New York. Robb says it was only a massage. Chuck Robb lived a lie and violated his oath of good faith to the people." A Robb ad countered that "North's public record includes putting himself above the law by selling arms to terrorists and back-dating documents to conceal that some of the money went for his personal use. Oliver North—people are starting to wonder if he knows what the truth is." Another Robb ad began "After lying about President Reagan and even lying to schoolchildren, Oliver North is lying about Chuck Robb."[30]

Although Republicans sought to foster cynicism about the current state of government, believing correctly that it would hurt Democrats more than Republicans, it may ultimately come back to haunt them. One *Doonesbury* cartoon drawn by Garry Trudeau soon after the election illustrated this.

Republicans and Democrats alike believe that the Republican majority's success in reforming Congress and in passing policies that appeal to the public will be critical factors in determining the longevity of the party's dominance. If Republicans are successful in passing popular legislation and Clinton remains unpopular, then the 1996 elections may mark the solidification of the "rolling realignment." Newt Gingrich (R-Georgia) cautions, however, that if in two years the public believes that the Republicans have not governed better than Democrats had, their majority status will be seriously threatened. Whether that would result in a shift toward the Democrats, or in increasing calls for independent candidacies, remains to be seen.

THE NEW CONGRESS

Although the partisan balance of the new House and Senate differs from that of past years, the new members in other ways resemble those they replace. The demographic profile of newly elected members is remarkably similar to that of previous years. In the year after the "Year of the Woman," the number of women in Congress increased slightly, with some Democratic pro-choice women losing to Republican pro-life women challengers. Professor Sue Thomas of Georgetown University, an expert on women in legislatures, noted that "suggestions that this small gain is meaningless

TABLE 3

Characteristics of the 104th Congress

	HOUSE	SENATE
Average Age	50.9	58.4
Women	49	8
African Americans	39	1
Hispanics	18	0
Asians/Pacific Islanders	6	2
Native Americans	0	1
PRINCIPAL OCCUPATIONS		
Law	170	54
Business or banking	163	24
Politics/Public service	102	12
Education	76	10
Real estate	28	3
Journalism	15	8
Agriculture	19	9
Engineering	6	0
Medicine	10	1
Homemaker	1	0
Clergy	2	0
RELIGIOUS AFFILIATIONS		
Mainline Protestants	153	47
Evangelical Protestants	72	10
Unspecified Protestants	38	3
Mormon	10	3
Roman Catholic	125	20
Jewish	24	9

SOURCE: Supplement to *Congressional Quarterly Weekly Report,* Nov. 12, 1994, pp. 9–12. Reprinted by permission.

compared with those in 1992 miss the larger point—that the Republican sweep was not synonymous with women losing ground that they had so recently gained and long sought. Women proved that they can make gains in both parties."

Table 3 (on p. 35) shows some characteristics of the new Congress. The new Congress has proportionately fewer lawyers than the 103rd, and comparatively more businesswomen and -men. Fewer of the new members have held previous public office than in past Congresses, primarily because of the success of Republican business executives who launched their political careers with a run for the House.

In one respect, the new Congress differs substantially from the one that served four years earlier. More than half of Republican members and nearly a third of Democrats are in their first or second term, making the 104th Congress one of the least experienced on record. Many of these new members are committed to changing the way that Congress does its business.

Republicans Clean House

In an effort to prove that they can govern better, Republicans quickly began to adopt procedural and structural reforms. In the summer before the 1994 elections, Newt Gingrich assembled a team of House Republicans

Wide World Photos

Marking the start of the Republican revolution set in motion by voters in November 1994, House members were sworn into the 104th Congress in the House Chambers on Capitol Hill on Wednesday, January 4, 1995.

to plan a strategy should the Republicans win a majority. Since the majority party in the House has great latitude in organizing the chamber, the team planned major reforms in the way that the House would carry out business.

Senate Republicans made no such pledge. One reason for this difference lies in the institutional rules and histories of the House and Senate. For forty years Democrats in the House have used a somewhat rigid set of rules and a comfortable majority to deny Republicans access to policymaking. Although Republicans were invited to the official committee meetings including the important "mark-up" sessions in which the language of legislation is revised, in practice Democrats frequently agreed on language in private negotiations held in closed sessions, then used their majority to pass the party language in committee. Rules passed by the Democratic majority on the House Rules Committee prevented Republicans from offering amendments on the floor.

In contrast, relationships between Republicans and Democrats in the Senate have been more cordial. The Senate does much of its business through unanimous consent, and allows the minority party to block legislation through the filibuster. The Democratic majority was in constant negotiation with the Republicans on the content of legislation, and was generally powerless to pass bills without at least some Republican support. Moreover, the Republicans controlled the Senate from 1980 through 1986, and depended on the support of at least some Democratic senators to pass their legislative agenda.

Committee Reforms in the House

Because Gingrich wanted to devote the first 100 days of the 104th Congress to enacting the legislation promised in the "Contract with America," House Republicans scrambled to quickly adopt legislative reforms. Their party caucus hashed out organizational changes, with the understanding that the party would vote as a bloc to enact the changes at the start of the legislative session. The changes in House organization and rules will constitute the most sweeping reforms since the 1946 Legislative Reorganization Act.

House Republicans eliminated three committees and a number of subcommittees, reduced the number of members who serve on each committee, slashed committee staff by one-third, and imposed six-year term limits on committee and subcommittee chairs. Table 4 (on p. 38) shows the downscaling of size and jurisdictions of committees in the new Congress. Republicans promised to eliminate 25 of the 115 subcommittees as well, but left the details of this reduction to be worked out later. Democrats had previously eliminated 16 subcommittees in 1993.

The Republicans also renamed some committees, in part to modernize the chamber—as the committee names were 50 years old—and in part to

TABLE 4

House Committee Names, Sizes, and Jurisdictions[*]

	1993-94		1994–95		CHANGE
Agriculture	27D	19R	26R	21D	+1
Appropriations	37D	23R	31R	21D	-14
Banking and Financial Services *(formerly Banking, Finance, and* *Urban Affairs—jurisdiction expanded)*	30D	20R 1I	25R	21D	-5
Budget	26D	17R	24R	20D	+1
Commerce *(formerly Energy and Commerce—* *jurisdiction narrowed)*	27D	17R	25R	21D	-2
Economic Opportunity *(formerly Education and Labor)*	24D	15R	19R	16D	-4
Government Reform and Oversight *(formerly Government Operations—* *jurisdiction expanded)*	25D	16R 1I	21R	17D	-4
House Oversight *(formerly House Administration)*	12D	7R	5R	3D	-11
International Relations *(formerly Foreign Affairs)*	26D	18R	21R	18D	-5
Judiciary	21D	14R	20R	15D	0
National Security *(formerly Armed Services—jurisdiction* *expanded)*	33D	22R	27R	23D	-5
Public Lands and Resources *(formerly Natural Resources—* *jurisdiction expanded)*	24D	15R	19R	16D	-4
Rules	9D	4R	9R	4D	0
Select Intelligence	12D	7R	8R	6D	-5
Small Business	27D	18R	19R	16D	-10
Standards of Official Conduct	7D	7R	7R	7D	0
Technology and Competitiveness *(formerly Science, Space, and* *Technology—jurisdiction expanded)*	33D	22R	27R	23D	-5
Transportation and Infrastructure *(formerly Public Works and Trans-* *portation—jurisdiction expanded)*	38D	25R	31R	27D	-5
Veterans' Affairs	21D	14R	17R	14D	-4
Ways and Means	24D	14R	21R	14D	-3

[*]Committees on the District of Columbia, the Merchant Marines and Fisheries, and the Post Office and Civil Service were eliminated.

reflect their new legislative priorities. The old Banking, Finance, and Urban Affairs Committee was renamed Banking and Financial Services, reflecting a decreased emphasis on urban matters. The Education and Labor Committee is now called Economic Opportunity, a move that Republicans said reflected their desire to shift most education matters to the states and to symbolize that while Democrats support organized labor, Republicans create opportunities for ordinary Americans. The Committee on Natural Resources was renamed Public Lands and Resources, reflecting Republican emphasis on development and exploitation of natural resources in contrast to the Democratic emphasis on protecting the environment.[31]

Committee jurisdictions changed as well. The most significant reduction targeted Energy and Commerce, henceforth to be called the Commerce Committee. Under a powerful chair, John Dingell (D-Michigan), this committee once had partial control over 40 percent of all legislation in the House. Republicans removed jurisdiction over railroads and inland waterways (to Transportation and Infrastructure), the Trans-Alaska Pipeline (to Public Lands and Resources), the Glass-Steagall Act (to Banking and Financial Services), inspection of seafood (to Agriculture), and energy research and development (to Technology and Competitiveness).

The diverse nature of the issues removed from the Commerce Committee is a testimony to the ability of powerful chairs to expand committee jurisdictions over time. Many Democrats as well as Republicans welcomed the changes, including Lee Hamilton (D-Indiana), co-chair of the Joint Committee on the Organization of Congress.

David Dreier (R-California), who devised and negotiated these changes, initially sought even larger changes. Five committees were targeted for elimination—District of Columbia, Merchant Marines and Fisheries, Post Office and Civil Service, Small Business, and Veterans' Affairs. The first three were ultimately eliminated, the latter two were not. Thomas Mann, a congressional scholar at the Brookings Institution, notes that "the three committees that were eliminated have Democratic constituencies, and the two that weren't eliminated have Republican constituencies." Dreier also originally proposed to move jurisdiction over ethics issues from the Standards of Official Conduct Committee (which has equal numbers of Democrats and Republicans) to the partisan House Oversight Committee. This plan became politically delicate because of ongoing investigations by the ethics panel into a possible connection between Gingrich's political action committee (GOPAC) and a college course he taught at Kennesaw State College.

Dreier had also initially promised to sharply reduce the jurisdiction of the Energy and Commerce Committee, but although the list of jurisdiction changes may appear long, the overall impact will be minor. Dennis Fitzgibbons, spokesperson for outgoing Energy and Commerce Chair John Dingell, argued that "the significant areas where the committee has legislated in the past won't be changed very much." The new Commerce Committee will remain one of the most important in the House, a testimony to the negotiating skills of incoming chair Thomas Bliley (R-Virginia), who opposed the deep cuts initially proposed by Dreier.

Committee Reforms in the Senate

Republicans in the Senate responded to the House reforms by promising their own reductions in committee and personal staff, and appointing a task force to produce an unspecified but comprehensive committee reform package by March 1, 1995. Pete Domenici (R-New Mexico) and Connie Mack (R-Florida) indicated that they would also propose the elimination of some committees.

The changes in committee jurisdiction and chairs suggest some important adjustments in policy priorities of the new Congress. Jurisdiction over the Trans-Alaska Pipeline was transferred to the Natural Resources Committee, and the new chair of that panel, Don Young (R-Alaska), is a proponent of opening Alaskan wilderness to oil exploration. The chair of the Senate Energy and Natural Resources Committee is Frank Murkowski (R-Alaska), also a proponent of the development of this pristine territory.

Incoming House Commerce Committee Chair Thomas Bliley of Virginia will have control over a panel that is charged with the regulation of tobacco. Subcommittee chair Henry Waxman (D-California) held a series

Wide World Photos

New Commerce Committee Chair Thomas Bliley (R-Virginia)
favors decreased regulation of business in general and makes no
secret about his support for the tobacco industry in particular.
His congressional office is decorated with pictures of every brand
of cigarette produced by Philip Morris.

of highly publicized hearings in 1993 and 1994 that appeared likely to lead to an eventual recommendation that the government regulate nicotine as an addictive drug. Bliley represents a tobacco-growing district, and is likely to quash any further hearings. In response to Bliley's selection, the cartoonist Garry Trudeau launched a series of *Doonesbury* strips portraying "Mr. Butts," a huge cigarette representing tobacco companies, being feted in the new committee.

In addition to changes in committees, the Republicans have also announced that they will eliminate funding for twenty-eight congressional caucuses, which previously had received taxpayer dollars. The announcement was immediately denounced by a number of caucus leaders, including Kweisi Mfume of the Congressional Black Caucus, who had initially been very responsive to Republican overtures on some issues.

Dianne C. Lambert, an expert on congressional caucuses, noted that the Republican proposal will not save any taxpayer money, for the money will simply revert to office funds. Members will then be able to use the funds to pay for membership dues in the caucuses, which will rise as some of the caucuses move off the Hill and open new offices.

Procedural Reforms

In addition to changes in the committee structure, Republicans propose to change the way Congress operates as well. They plan to prohibit proxy voting in committees, a common practice for many years. Because challengers can use the incumbents' missed votes as an election issue, this reform will create a strong incentive for members to attend committee and subcommittee meetings. Moreover, since members can only be in one meeting at a time, it is also expected to reduce the number of committee and subcommittee hearings.

For many years Democrats have passed restrictive rules that limited Republican (and Democratic) amendments to key legislation. Republicans have promised to allow open rules on most major legislation, which would allow any member to offer amendments to the core of the Republican agenda. Some scholars see this strategy as a recipe for disaster. Given the narrow Republican majority, they argue, such a change would almost certainly doom some of the Republican contract to defeat. Democrats will be able to offer key amendments to major legislation that might entice sufficient numbers of Republicans to alter or even defeat legislation. Steven S. Smith, a political scientist who has written on congressional committees, argued that "I can't see how they can possibly do that [vote on the 10 parts of the Contract] if they don't control the floor agenda through special rules. The Democrats aren't dumb, after all. They'll find ways to pick apart those Republican bills if left unchecked."[32]

But incoming Rules Committee chair Gerald B. F. Solomon (R-New York) promised "fair rules . . . free and open debate. We're going to let the

House work its will."[33] Republicans have argued that the Democrats needed closed rules because Republican amendments were especially attractive to southern Democratic moderates, and therefore endangered the party's majority. Republicans, they believe, are more unified and therefore less vulnerable to such tactics. "We don't have a fractionalized situation," said Solomon, "I can afford to be even more fair than you would be under normal circumstances."[34] As of late January 1995, however, the Republicans had yet to allow open rules.

Such a change would depend in part on the ability of members of both parties to maintain civility. Over the past two decades, partisan differences in the House have become more bitter. Republicans frequently offered divisive amendments on issues such as abortion, which slowed the pace of legislative action and forced Democrats to cast votes they found difficult to defend in their districts. As a consequence, Democrats increasingly reverted to a set of rules designed to limit the number and nature of amendments. The success of the Republican "open rule" strategy will depend on whether the Democrats adopt the aggressive tactics practiced by the former Republican minority. Smith predicts that "when the Democrats start to realize the potential of floor amendments, they're going to cause many of those Republicans in marginal districts a lot of pain."[35] If Smith is right, partisan maneuvering may sink the open rules.

Party Leadership in the New Congress

As expected, House Republicans selected Newt Gingrich as Speaker by acclamation. The *Washington Post* compared Gingrich's selection to a football rally, and reported that Gingrich's supporters chanted "Newt! Newt! Newt!" after his election. Republicans also elected Richard Armey (R-Texas) as majority leader by voice vote, and selected Tom DeLay (R-Texas) as majority whip. This Republican leadership team (shown in Table 5 along with other major leadership positions) is comprised of members with very conservative policy views and a commitment to activist leadership.

House Democrats surprised many observers by reelecting their leadership team of Dick Gephardt (D-Missouri) and David Bonior (D-Michigan) in contested elections against two conservative southern Democrats. New York Representative Gary Ackerman told reporters that the Democrats were angry with outgoing Speaker Tom Foley, not with Gephardt or Bonior. He noted that Foley, who kept the House in session long after many members wanted to return home to campaign, "didn't know it was time to go home and campaign for himself or the rest of us." But southern Democrats voiced displeasure with the choices, arguing that the party leadership was too liberal.

Senate Republicans chose Robert Dole (R-Kansas) to serve as Majority Leader, a post he held in the 1980s when the Republicans last held a majority. They chose Trent Lott (R-Mississippi) over former Minority Whip

TABLE 5		
Major Leadership Positions in 104th Congress		

HOUSE REPUBLICANS

Speaker	Newt Gingrich, R-Ga.
Majority Leader	Richard K. Armey, R-Tex.
Majority Whip	Tom D. DeLay, R-Tex.

HOUSE DEMOCRATS

| Minority Leader | Richard Gephardt, D-Mo. |
| Minority Whip | David E. Bonior, D-Mich. |

SENATE REPUBLICANS

| Majority Leader | Robert Dole, R-Kan. |
| Minority Leader | Trent Lott, R-Miss. |

SENATE DEMOCRATS

| Minority Leader | Tom Daschle, D-S.Dak. |
| Minority Whip | Wendell Ford, D-Ky. |

Alan Simpson (R-Wyoming) as Majority Whip, however, signaling support for a more conservative and aggressive policy. Lott was an ally of Gingrich when he served in the House in the early 1980s, and is likely to advocate many of the programs contained in the Contract, whereas Simpson has long been a target of pro-life Republicans because of his support for reproductive rights. In a generational contest, Senate Democrats chose the relative newcomer Tom Daschle (D-South Dakota) as majority leader over Christopher Dodd (D-Connecticut) and reelected Wendell Ford (D-Kentucky) as party whip.

The Powers of the Speaker

Although House Republicans will probably not change the formal powers of House leadership, it is likely that Newt Gingrich will exercise far more control of the House than former speaker Tom Foley. Indeed, Gingrich may become more powerful than any Speaker in many years. Gingrich is a man with a vision who believes that he is destined to play a "transformational" role in an American political revolution that will save America from enemies within and without. Whereas Foley was content to negotiate and conciliate, Gingrich is likely to seek to mold legislation.

Newt Gingrich: Can the Revolutionary Lead?

Wide World Photos

Newt Gingrich has leaped from virtual obscurity to the position of (in Time *magazine's words) virtual president. In the weeks after his election and inauguration, Gingrich was in the news every day in connection with stories ranging from his 4.5-million-dollar book deal, to what his mother was saying about Hillary Clinton, to his marathon first session, which came to an end at 1:45 A.M.*

Newt Gingrich is a former history professor who believes that there are certain periods when the course of history can be dramatically changed by one man. He sees himself as destined to lead America in a new revolution that will protect it from enemies abroad and at home. In January of 1994, Gingrich gave voice to the urgency he feels: "I don't want my country to collapse. I don't want my daughter and wife raped and killed. I don't want to see my neighborhood destroyed. People like me are what stand between us and Auschwitz. I see evil around me every day."[36]

Gingrich began planning how the Republicans could take control of the House of Representatives soon after his election in 1978. He argued that they needed to portray the Democratic party as corrupt and dangerous, and the Republicans as the party of hope. Although House Republicans in the 1970s principally did business by bargaining with Democrats, Gingrich instead advocated direct confrontation.

Gingrich put this advice into action almost immediately. He instituted the practice of making late-afternoon speeches to an empty House chamber in which he denounced Democrats and even challenged them to answer his charges. The television camera focused only on the speaker, so viewers were unaware that Gingrich was addressing an empty chamber. This created the misleading impression that Gingrich's arguments cowed the Democrats, who in fact were simply not present. House Speaker Tip O'Neill was so angered by one Gingrich speech that he ordered the cameras to pan across the empty chamber during the next session. He then rebuked Gingrich publicly, only to have his words stricken from the record.

In 1989, Gingrich won a surprising victory in an election for party whip against a moderate Republican backed by the party leadership, in part because of Republican anger over the partisan tactics of then-Speaker Jim Wright (D-Texas). Gingrich's complaint against Wright for violation of House honoraria limits eventually led to his resignation, and earned Gingrich the gratitude of many Republicans. Gingrich also began playing a major role in recruiting and funding House challengers, and many of the junior Republicans in the House remember his campaign advice and aid.

During the past decade, Gingrich's elections in his district have been uncomfortably close because of his ability to both infuriate Democrats and alienate moderate Republicans. Georgians reacted negatively to Gingrich's vote in favor of a pay raise, his bounced checks during the House banking scandal, and his chauffeur-driven limousine.

Gingrich is the most controversial figure to achieve the Speaker's position in recent times, and it is likely that the media will have a field day pointing to his inconsistencies and idiosyncrasies. Although Gingrich won his first election on a theme of family values, his first wife recounts that soon after his victory he confronted her in the hospital where she was being treated for cancer, pulled out a note pad, and began discussing the terms of their divorce, an image that inspired a *Doonesbury* cartoon series soon after the 1994 elections. His soon-to-be-published science fiction novel *1945* drew widespread media attention for its steamy sex scenes and its description of a "goofy" George Bush, a reference that was later dropped. The media are also likely to begin to hold Gingrich responsible for his rhetorical excesses. The facts and examples from Gingrich's speeches frequently do not stand up to public scrutiny, and soon after the election, *Time* magazine published a list of his recent factual errors.

In January 1995, Gingrich became embroiled in a controversy that resembled the one he had used to bring down Wright. Gingrich announced that he had signed a book contract that would pay him a $4.5-million advance with a publishing firm owned by Rupert Murdoch, who had billions of dollars at stake in telecommunications business pending before the federal government. After a storm of controversy,

Gingrich instead accepted a $1 advance, but his private meetings with Murdoch led Democrats to charge that Gingrich's deal was a form of access buying.

Gingrich's aggressive partisan style was well-suited to mobilize party anger. During the 1994 election, he advised Republican candidates to use "contrast words" such as "decay, failure, shallow, traitors, pathetic, corrupt, incompetent, and sick" in characterizing their Democratic opponents. His verbal attacks on Clinton and other Democrats have been steeped in such rhetoric. Yet to achieve the goals outlined in the Contract, Gingrich will need to bargain with the president, and with moderate Republicans in the Senate for whom he has occasionally also had some harsh words.

Gingrich's rhetoric after the election gave mixed signals concerning his ability to moderate his tone. He promised to work with the president, and had generally kind words for departing Speaker Tom Foley, but he also charged that up to a quarter of the White House staff had engaged in recent use of illegal drugs (although Gingrich himself has admitted to smoking marijuana in the past), and described the Clinton White House as "counterculture McGoverniks" and "left-wing elitists." Great revolutionaries often turn out to be unskilled at the art of governing. Whether Gingrich can make the transition remains to be seen.

Gingrich has resources at his disposal to do so. Foley negotiated with established, experienced committee chairs whose legislative turf was clearly defined, but Gingrich played a key role in the definition of committee jurisdiction, and the selection of committee chairs. Although Republican party rules give the party leader the power to select twelve of the twenty-three members of the Steering Committee, which appoints members and chairs of committees, Gingrich exercised far more authority than the formal rules would suggest. In a power move unseen in the House since the days of "Uncle Joe" Cannon at the turn of the century, he announced his choices for committee chairs in advance of any Steering Committee decisions, in several cases bypassing more senior members of a particular committee to select an individual who shared his policy views. Moreover, Gingrich indicated that he might seek to remove committee chairs who opposed his legislative agenda.

In the former Democratic House, committees controlled the substance of the legislative agenda. Committees were the repositories of expertise, both because of their sizable professional staff and because their chairs had served for many years and had gradually mastered the substance of the issues. When legislation passed a major committee, it generally received a closed rule and passed on the floor of the House largely unmodified. The new rules are designed in part to weaken committees, giving them fewer professional staff with which to dominate the technical discussion, and imposing term limits on committee and subcommittee chairs to prevent them from establishing entrenched power bases. This should allow the party leadership to assume a larger role in molding the content of legislation.

It is likely that Gingrich will be able to dominate the House in the first year or two of Republican control. House Republicans are a remarkably junior lot, with over half of them in their first or second term, and nearly 70 percent elected since Gingrich took over GOPAC and began actively campaigning for Republican candidates across the country.

When Gingrich took over GOPAC from then-senator Pierre "Pete" DuPont (R-Delaware) in 1979, the organization limited its activities to funding candidates for state and local elections. Gingrich expanded the activities of the organization to include candidate recruitment and training. He produced a number of audio- and videotapes which were distributed to candidates, schooling them on important issues and campaign techniques, and offering inspirational messages. Many junior Republicans gratefully recall Gingrich's inspiration and efforts, and most give him credit for transforming the Republican party from a permanent minority into the majority. Congressional expert Norman Ornstein notes that to some House Republicans, Gingrich is like Moses, who led his people to the promised land after 40 years in the wilderness.[37]

Wide World Photos

Senate Majority Leader Robert Dole meets with Republican members of Congress. Dole has been cultivating his image as a statesman, a role he will have to play to foster unity among his majority in the Senate and keep alive his hopes for a future presidential candidacy.

Yet over time, Gingrich's aggressive leadership style may create friction. Congress is designed to work in committees, and committee chairs and subcommittee chairs are powerful figures even if their terms are limited. It is doubtful that a Speaker can thoroughly dominate a decentralized body like the House for a substantial period of time. Should Republicans maintain a majority in the House over several sessions, it seems likely that power will flow back to the committees. Indeed, committee chairs have already voiced skepticism over some of Gingrich's proposals. For example, Representative Henry Hyde (R-Illinois), chair of the Judiciary Committee, has indicated disapproval of the proposed rule requiring a 60 percent majority to approve tax increases.

In the Senate, in contrast, House Majority Leader Robert Dole will face a set of powerful, experienced senators, many of whom have served as committee chairs between 1980 and 1986. Moreover, the informal rules in the Senate, the use of unanimous consent, and the threat of a filibuster even within the majority party all mean that Dole must carefully consult with members of his own party in crafting legislative compromise. In addition, because Senate Republicans are far short of the sixty votes needed to end a Democratic filibuster, Dole will need to negotiate with conservative Democrats as well.

THE REPUBLICAN AGENDA

The House Republican agenda dominated debate in Washington after the election. Gingrich's promise to vote on the legislation that is described in the "Contract with America" in the first 100 days is likely to enable him to control the agenda for at least that long. In the early months of 1995, Congress and the president will principally respond to the legislation that embodies the promises of the Contract.

The "Contract with America"

The Contract is an ambitious program that includes some legislation that is likely to be popular and some that will prove to be quite controversial. Although Republicans hold narrow majorities in both the House and Senate, it is unlikely that all of the Contract will become law. First, not all Republicans support the entire plan, and Senate Republicans in particular may object to some elements. Second, Democrats in the Senate can filibuster parts of the package that they oppose, and if House Republicans allow open rules on these major bills, House Democrats will be able to build coalitions to amend major portions of the bills. Finally, Republicans are far short of the needed votes to override a presidential veto. Nonetheless, Gingrich has promised to read the Contract aloud on the floor of the House every day until all elements have been voted on. Let us consider what the Republicans seek to accomplish.

"The Fiscal Responsibility Act"

The "Contract with America" promised to reform the way that the House operates. It promised a vote on a Balanced Budget Amendment and on a line-item veto, both intended to curb congressional spending. The proposed constitutional amendment would require Congress to balance the federal budget every year beginning in fiscal year 2002, or the second year after the amendment is ratified by three-fourths of the states. Congress could escape the provisions with a three-fifths vote of both the House and Senate, or in times of war or a serious national security threat. Clinton opposes such an amendment, but the joint resolution used for constitutional amendments will not require his signature.

If ratified by the states, the Balanced Budget Amendment would demand more centralization of budgeting in Congress and require some very hard choices of members in both chambers. The budget deficit is projected to reach $181,077,000 in fiscal year 1999, and closing it would require either deep cuts in spending, additional revenues, or both. Moreover, the Contract includes tax cuts that would lose additional revenue. Some budget analysts estimate that if Republican tax-cut plans pass and Republicans keep their pledge to maintain current levels of defense spending and Social Security benefits, the remainder of the domestic budget will have to be cut by 43 percent in order to balance the budget. Some form of a balanced budget amendment may pass in 1995, but the House Republican version, which would require a three-fifths vote for tax increases, would make it difficult to raise revenue. In January 1995, Senator Robert Byrd (D-West Virginia) began a filibuster of the balanced budget amendment in the Senate, demanding that the Republicans specify the program cuts they would make to balance the budget. Dole warned that the Senate would not approve the amendment if it contained the super-majority provision for tax hikes. And Republican governors insisted that Congress first pass legislation guaranteeing that the costs of the cuts would not be passed on to the states.

Clinton has long supported a line-item veto, which would enable any president to veto specific spending items from appropriations bills or tax breaks for specific groups from revenue bills. Congress would have twenty days to vote by simple majority to disapprove the president's veto, after which time the president could exercise it again. To override this second veto, Congress would need the traditional two-thirds vote in both chambers.

The line-item veto would change the balance of power between Congress and the president by allowing the president to eliminate specific programs from appropriations bills. This power, which many governors exercise, would greatly increase the bargaining ability of a president with members of Congress. Currently presidents lack a credible threat to entice members to support their legislation, but with a line-item veto a president could deny appropriations targeted to particular states or congressional districts, thus pressuring individual members of Congress. Moreover, presidents could effectively kill programs by refusing them funding.

"The Taking Back Our Streets Act"

Another part of the platform is a promise to revise the crime bill to eliminate many of the crime prevention programs—which many Republicans label as "pork"—and transfer those funds into prison construction. The plan would also limit the legal right to appeal of death-row inmates. Exit polls showed voters to be greatly concerned with violent crime, so many of these proposals should be popular. But Republican efforts to eliminate crime prevention programs may encounter resistance from police organizations. Some Republicans also seek to repeal the ban on assault weapons, although that is not part of the Contract. That proposal would likely generate a good deal of opposition from across the political spectrum.

"The Personal Responsibility Act"

Republicans promised to make sharp changes in the programs that provide cash and food to poor families. The proposals would ban Aid to Families with Dependent Children (AFDC) benefits to children born to unwed mothers under age 18, and allow states to raise that to age 21. The savings from these reduced AFDC benefits would go to the states in bloc grants to enable them to build orphanages, to promote adoption, and operate residential group homes for unwed mothers. Welfare benefits would also not increase for mothers who have additional children, and all mothers would be required to establish paternity before receiving AFDC.

Welfare recipients would be required to work an average of thirty-five hours per week in programs provided by the states, and all families' welfare benefits would be ended after five years. Overall anti-poverty program spending would be capped. Republicans would consolidate nutrition programs into a discretionary bloc grant to the states, which would allow states considerable freedom in defining their response to hunger.

Although there appears to be some elite consensus on welfare reform, the specifics of this program seem likely to be controversial. Catholic bishops have announced their opposition to limits on payments to support children on the grounds that they may lead poor women to obtain abortions. Some Republicans want to go much further than the proposal, eliminating most programs to help the poor. Senate Republicans are likely to seek to soften the plan, especially the proposal to fold food stamps into a

Wide World Photos

The Poor People's Congress gathers in front of the Capitol building in late 1994 to protest the proposed welfare reform contained in the Republican "Contract with America."

discretionary bloc grant. Farm-state senators (including Dole) have long favored the food stamp program, which provides nutrition for the needy and helps support farm prices in the process. President Clinton, who promised welfare reform during his 1992 campaign, will probably seek to be an active player in molding this legislation.

The Republican welfare reform plan attracted a good deal of controversy in the months after the election. Shortly before Christmas, Newt Gingrich appeared on magazine covers portrayed variously as the "Gingrich Who Stole Christmas" or as Ebenezer Scrooge, who, when confronted with the poor on the streets, cried, "What, are there no orphanages?"

Although reductions in welfare are likely to be popular with voters, opponents will seek to portray the Republican plan as heartless, for it denies benefits to poor children. Mothers whose benefits expire and who cannot work would receive no cash aid. *Newsweek* estimated that if Gingrich's plan were in full effect today, more than half of the nearly 10 million children who now depend on AFDC would be denied benefits. Although Republicans hope that most of these children will be cared for by relatives or private charities, many would end up in the orphanages that states would be allowed (but not required) to build. Such orphanages would be far more expensive than AFDC (*Newsweek* reported that one program spent nearly $60,000 per child per year), and the image of taking young children away from poor mothers and moving them to public institutions is likely to be a controversial one. One poll in *Time* magazine reported that a clear majority of Americans opposed eliminating welfare benefits for mothers with children who had unsuccessfully tried to find work, and that an even larger majority favored additional programs in job training over the Republican emphasis on slashing benefits. By mid-January 1995, Republicans were considering a proposal to consolidate all welfare programs into bloc grants and allow states to make their own decisions about eligibility and benefit levels. Such a proposal had the obvious advantage of passing responsibility to state governors and legislatures. Senator Nancy Kassebaum (R-Kansas) proposed that the federal government simply assume responsibility for Medicaid, which is currently funded by the states, and allow the states to use the savings to design their own welfare programs.

This decentralized approach would likely mean that poor citizens in one state might receive food, housing, and cash assistance while citizens in identical circumstances in another state received no state aid. It is highly unlikely that the Republican plan will pass in 100 days, although it may inspire a spirited debate and ultimately lead to some form of welfare reform.

"The Family Reinforcement Act"

Republicans have drafted a Family Reinforcement Act, which would increase penalties for child pornography and sexual abuse and grant families a tax credit for caring for an elderly parent or grandparent, or for adopting a child. The credits will cost about $9 billion by Republican estimates, and their fate may hinge on the ability of proponents to find a way to pay for them. Some Republicans have pushed to include vouchers to pay for education at either public or private schools, although current drafts of the act do not include that controversial proposal, in part because of the opposition of some key Republicans.

"The American Dream Restoration Act"

Republicans promised tax breaks for the middle class, including an additional $500 tax credit for families earning up to $200,000 a year, a tax credit to eliminate the marriage penalty, and a new kind of Individual Retirement Account (IRA) which would require taxes to be paid on the income put into the account but not on the interest it accrued. As usual, the Republican plan immediately triggered a bidding war, with House Minority Leader Richard Gephardt (D-Missouri) and President Clinton each offering somewhat different proposals. The Democratic plans would extend the tax break to families with incomes under $75,000 and set up a partisan debate over whether families with incomes of $200,000 need an expensive tax break. Republicans estimate that the proposal would cost the government more than $107 billion over five years.

Although politicians on both sides of the fence had a bad case of tax-cut fever in late 1994, economists were less enthusiastic about the concept. Interest rates rose steadily throughout 1994, and increased spending by consumers and a possibly larger budget deficit would likely drive rates still higher, hurting the middle class. Senate Republicans are leery of any legislation that would increase the national debt, and Republicans may find that passing $107 billion in spending cuts is a tougher proposition than they think. House Republicans have hinted that cuts in road building, cancer research, and environmental cleanup would finance the cuts.

"The National Security Restoration Act"

Republicans have drafted a National Security Restoration Act to restrict the use of United States forces in U.N. missions, to ensure significant levels of defense spending, and to help expand NATO. The bill would ban the use of United States troops under foreign command unless the president certified in writing that the mission was central to national defense. It would also renew a commitment to a national missile defense, and commit the United States to an expansion of NATO.

"The Senior Citizens Fairness Act"

Republicans proposed a package of benefits to senior citizens that would allow them to earn more income without losing Social Security payments, to repeal the taxes which were passed in 1993 on Social Security benefits of wealthy retirees, and to create tax incentives to encourage individuals to purchase private long-term care insurance. These proposals would also cost the government a significant amount, and so will encounter some resistance from Senate Republicans, but there will certainly be strong pressure from interest groups that represent the elderly to cut taxes on Social Security payments for higher income retirees.

"The Job Creation and Wage Enhancement Act"

Coupled with the modest cuts for the middle class is a promise of a reduction of the taxes on capital gains—the profits made from the sale of stocks, bonds, and real estate. The Contract calls for cutting the tax rate on capital gains in half, and then indexing the value of the asset to inflation. Because this tax cut would primarily benefit the wealthiest Americans, it will face the threat of a filibuster in the Senate and a presidential veto. A carefully crafted capital-gains reduction could become law, however.

This bill will also contain a variety of provisions making it more difficult for government to pass new regulations that affect business profits, and will limit the government's ability to act in ways that reduce the value of private property. These latter proposals will be strongly opposed by environmentalists and other liberal groups, and may also face a veto.

"The Common Sense Legal Reform Act"

Republicans propose to cap the amount of punitive damages that juries can award in product liability and medical malpractice suits, and to allow judges to require the loser to pay legal fees for the winning side. Republicans argue that their proposal would reduce frivolous litigation and outrageous awards. Democrats counter that it would make it difficult for poor or middle-class citizens to file suit. Clinton may veto this package unless it is carefully crafted.

"The Citizen Legislature Act"

House Republicans pledged to vote on term limits in the first 100 days of 1995, but soon after the election some Republican leaders began to dis-

Reuters/Bettmann

Dick Armey exemplifies the inevitable switch in thinking that accompanies incumbency. Shortly after the elections, Armey told reporters that the Republicans had merely pledged a vote on term limits, without promising to pass them.

tance themselves from the idea. Term limits seemed especially attractive in past elections to Republicans who sought any means to break the Democratic hold on Congress, but may seem counterproductive to those same members once they have achieved majority status. After laboring for many years with little opportunity to affect national legislation, some Republicans now find the thought of relinquishing power in a few years disconcerting. Indeed, soon after the election Majority Leader Dick Armey (R-Texas), once a proponent of term limits, argued that the 1994 elections may signal that limits are *not* needed, and repeatedly reminded reporters that the Contract only promised a *vote* on term limits, and did not promise to pass them. In contrast, President Clinton, who opposes term limits, quipped in a speech at Georgetown University soon after the elections that term limits were looking better and better.

The fate of term limits may be sealed by the U.S. Supreme Court, which heard arguments about the constitutionality of an Arkansas law in late November. In making its judgment, the Court will consider if term limits impose an additional qualification for office, thereby effectively amending the Constitution, or whether term limits are merely administrative regulations of elections that states have been allowed to impose, similar to barring convicts from office. If the Court rules that term limits are unconstitutional, it seems likely that the divisions within Republican ranks on the issue coupled with strong Democratic opposition would prevent passage of a constitutional amendment that would require a two-thirds majority to pass. If the Court allows such limits, however, then Congress will be able to enact term limits merely by passing legislation, although many senators and key House Republicans will oppose the legislation.

Social Issues

Although the Contract focuses primarily on procedural and economic policies, the most divisive issues for Republicans will be the social issues. Republicans are deeply divided on abortion, gay and lesbian rights, and the regulation of pornography. Some Republicans, including Gingrich, want to push for a school prayer amendment early in 1995; others seek additional restrictions on abortion or on civil rights for gay men and lesbians, and other programs backed by the Christian Right.[38]

Such proposals will surely prove divisive to Republicans. The newly elected House Republicans include members who support the agenda of the Christian Right as well as many libertarians who strongly oppose legislating morality. Moreover, any attempt to sharply restrict abortion rights or to push a moral agenda will be unpopular with many voters. The same election that produced a Republican majority found two statewide anti-gay referenda defeated in Oregon and Idaho, one pro-life referendum beaten in Wyoming, and doctor-assisted suicide approved in Oregon. Many Republicans hope to avoid the abortion issue altogether. Conservative strategist Bill Kristol advises pro-life Republicans that any attempt to pass strong pro-life legislation is doomed to fail. Yet with forty new pro-life members of the House—including six women—and nine of the eleven new senators opposing abortion, pro-life groups are anxious to press their agenda. Although most are willing to let the Republicans consider the "Contract with America" for the first 100 days, they will insist that abortion restrictions be considered soon afterwards.

The new Republicans in the House are generally quite conservative, but the small number of moderates may hold an important strategic position, for if they vote with Democrats they can defeat legislation. Some of the newly elected conservative members come from Democratic-leaning districts, and they may also defect to the Democrats on some legislation. In the Senate, moderate Republicans can join with Democrats to defeat legislation, and Democrats alone can filibuster a bill if they remain united. Gingrich may imagine a world in which a narrow majority can work its will, but the American system requires compromise at every step of the process.

Ultimately, the fate of the Republican agenda depends on the interrelations between various combinations of actors: the president and the Congress, the Senate and House Republicans, and congressional Democrats and Republicans.

Clinton and the New Republican Congress

The new Republican majorities in the House and Senate pose a major challenge to the Clinton administration. Clinton faces a problem much like the one faced by previous Republican presidents. For most of the last forty years, Republican presidents have faced a Democratic House of Representatives, and usually a Democratic Senate as well. Those Republican presidents learned that a Congress controlled by the opposition party frequently ignores or quickly defeats their pet legislation. None of Reagan's or Bush's budgets were taken seriously on Capitol Hill—indeed, a majority of House *Republicans* voted against them. Bush's top domestic priority, a capital gains tax cut, never came close to passing. Only by enlisting bipartisan support can presidents pass legislation through a Congress controlled by the opposing party.

For most of the first two years of his administration, Clinton pursued a largely partisan strategy, seeking votes primarily among Democrats and ignoring offers to negotiate by moderate Republicans. This strategy is no longer a viable one, for even if Clinton wins the vote of every Democrat, his legislation will fail. At the very least, the administration must reconstitute its legislative agenda, reconsider the positions it takes on key issues, and restructure its strategy for dealing with Congress. These are necessary

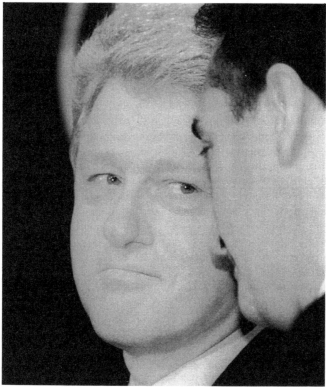

Reuters/Bettmann

An embattled President Clinton must meet with various advisers to determine strategies for dealing with Congress. Clinton could not persuade Congress to support all of his policies even when his fellow Democrats controlled the House and Senate.

but not easy tasks. They are necessary because the president can no longer control the legislative agenda, nor only pursue a partisan strategy, and can no longer prevent or contain potentially embarrassing congressional investigations. They are not easy because the president's governing coalition is small and divided and because the current political environment is hostile.

When confronted with a House and Senate dominated by Democrats, President Bush was content to concentrate primarily on foreign affairs. His chief of staff John Sununu told reporters relatively early in Bush's term that the best thing Congress could do was adjourn, for the administration wanted nothing else from them. This passive approach is unlikely to appeal to Clinton, whose campaign and political career has emphasized using the power of government to solve social and economic problems.

Thus, Clinton *must* deal with Congress. The issue is not whether he will do so but how—what legislative goals he will seek, what stands he will take on key issues, and what strategies he will employ.

President Clinton has several options. One is to confront Congress by sticking to the policy goals he favored before the midterm elections. These goals and the programs designed to achieve them are broadly consistent with his party's 1992 platform and his own campaign promises. They involve reducing crime, improving health care, reducing welfare dependency, protecting the environment, and encouraging investment, trade, and economic growth through increased government programs. Such an agenda is likely to continue to appeal to much of the president's electoral constituency. Liberal, and to a lesser extent, moderate Democrats generally approve of the job the president is doing and voted for Democratic candidates in the 1994 midterm elections. The agenda would also be consistent with the views of a majority of House Democrats whose center of gravity has moved to the left of the political spectrum with the resignation or defeat of moderate or conservative Democratic members of Congress.

Yet this agenda is unlikely to appeal to Republicans, whose votes are needed to pass legislation. The Republican "Contract with America" explicitly rejects much of this agenda and its pro-government orientation. Conservative Democrats also have reservations about some of these programs and would likely join their Republican colleagues to defeat Clinton's proposals. Indeed, Congress may simply ignore any presidential initiatives that involve additional government programs.

If Clinton cannot hope to realize many traditional Democratic proposals with the new Congress, he can derail the Republican program. Republican presidents who faced a Democratic Congress quickly learned to wield the veto, and more importantly, to use the *threat* of a veto in their negotiations with congressional leaders. Few presidential vetoes are overridden, giving presidents substantial bargaining power in the informal mark-up sessions that produce final legislation. The Democrats have ample strength to prevent a veto override, which requires a two-thirds vote of both houses.

Thus Clinton could choose to confront the Republican program directly, and block most of it from becoming law. A confrontational strategy has some potential political advantage for the president. It allows him to stand for something, thereby overcoming the perception that he lacks basic beliefs and fundamental principles. Moreover, if the Republicans do not deliver on their Contract, the president would be able to present a clear-cut alternative to the public, one that might have more appeal in 1996 after a "do-nothing" Republican Congress than it did in 1994 after a "do-little" Democratic one. In 1948, Harry Truman pursued this strategic approach successfully, and the White House staff began carefully studying the Truman campaign even before the election.

But there are political risks to adopting the Truman strategy.[39] When Truman ran against a "do-nothing" Republican Congress in 1948, a majority of Americans considered themselves Democrats. Today they do not, nor is the party unified behind Clinton's electoral agenda. Pollsters of both parties reported that the 1994 electorate wanted a smaller government, not additional programs. Moreover, presidents usually shoulder more blame for undesirable conditions and outcomes than does Congress or its individual members. Thus Clinton might engender more, not less, public disapproval were he to adopt this approach.

A second option is for the president to cooperate with Congress, at least at the outset. Were the president to do so he would have to redefine his policy agenda along more centrist lines. This might involve walking a tightrope between those policy positions that remain consistent with Democratic principles and interests and those that are more in line with the conservative mood of the electorate. A moderate group within the Democratic party, the Democratic Leadership Council, has urged him to do just that, to redefine what it means to be a "New Democrat."

Immediately after the election, Clinton sent strong signals that he will adopt this strategy. He gave a major speech at the Democratic Leadership Council in early December that won widespread praise from conservative Democrats. He also fired Surgeon General Joycelyn Elders, long a prime target of the right, for discussing the possibility that masturbation should be taught in schools.

Clinton may find that negotiating with Republicans will increase his popularity, and draw him toward the political center. His promise of welfare reform languished after congressional Democrats told him that it was unlikely to pass. In the 104th Congress, Clinton's welfare reform package seems genuinely centrist, and he has the opportunity to position himself as a president who seeks to reform the system while keeping children from hunger and homelessness.

If Clinton seeks to find common ground with the Republicans, however, he will almost certainly be accused of "selling out" to them by some elements within his party. The antipathy among liberal Democrats might be so great as to generate a liberal challenge to his renomination, as Bush was challenged by conservatives in 1988. The Reverend Jesse Jackson has already hinted at a possible independent candidacy. Given the president's low standing among most Republicans and many independents, it is unlikely that he would be reelected if he were weakened by a prenomination challenge and then had to contend with a splinter group from his party supporting an independent candidate in the general election.

Another problem with a cooperative approach is that it might muddy the waters and not provide for a clear policy choice in the next election. A lack of policy issues would enhance the importance of character issues which would probably not work to this president's political advantage. A strategy that involves a lot of compromises would undoubtedly make Clinton look weak and reinforce his politician image in an anti-politician era. Moreover, if the president pursued a common-ground strategy, he would have to do so initially on the basis of the Republicans' agenda, not his own. This would allow his opponents to choose the issues and define the terms of the debate, leaving the president to try to claim victory as best he could.

Finally, the cooperative approach may reinforce public perceptions that Clinton lacks core values. Clinton abandoned his pledge for a middle-class tax cut soon after his election, and told the nation that the deficit was a long-term threat to the middle class. In December 1994, however, Clinton announced his own variation on the Republican middle-class tax cut, and announced plans to cut spending to match. Although Clinton positioned himself to argue that his plan was more responsible than that of the Republicans, and more focused on the middle class, most political commentators responded negatively to the speech. Robert J. Samuelson, a noted economist and columnist, wrote that the president's tax-cut speech "had all the dignity of a home shopping program."

There is a third option, one that is not mutually exclusive of a confrontational or cooperative approach. This option would have the president emphasize those issues, perform those tasks, and exercise those powers that do not require much, if any, congressional involvement. Clinton would be an executive president employing that authority and influence that he can exercise alone. In the area of foreign and national security policy, for example, presidents have more discretion and frequently receive more public support when acting on behalf of the country. Using executive orders to make public policy in the absence of congressional action, as presidents have done in the area of civil rights, is another device that Clinton could employ to pursue aspects of his policy agenda. Finally, as an executive president, Clinton could take advantage of the ceremonial and symbolic aspects of the office to enhance his own status. Such an approach would not negate the legislature but would compete with it for public attention and, ultimately, public approval.

The political environment, the public mood, and external events will all impinge on what goals the president seeks, how he seeks them, and how successful he is apt to be. Clearly, the results of the 1994 midterm elections make it more difficult for President Clinton to exercise leadership, something that we expect all presidents to do. However, if there is a silver lining for the president in all of this, it is that public expectations will be lower for the president and will be higher for the Congress than they have been in recent years. Moreover, the president will now be compared to specific Republican leaders—the Speaker of the House, the Senate majority leader, and the next Republican presidential nominee—and not to some ideal president. Clinton should fare better by that comparison.

Ultimately, Clinton's relationship with Congress will hinge on his own strategic and political decisions, the public mood, and the activities of the Republican Congress. Some Republicans are very hostile toward the president, and cooperation with them will be difficult. Soon after the election, Senator Jesse Helms warned that the president's life would be in danger were he to visit a military base in North Carolina, a clear indication of Helms's dislike of Clinton. If Republicans spend a great deal of time on investigations of Whitewater and the Clinton administration, relations may become quickly strained. If, instead, the president and the Republicans become engaged in debates over how to reform welfare, how to restructure the tax code, and how to deal with issues such as health care and crime, both sides may benefit.

House and Senate Republicans

Although the House Republicans received the lion's share of attention after the 1994 election, Senate Republicans are playing a key role in shaping the legislative agenda in 1995. The Contract is essentially a House document, and a number of Senate Republicans have expressed skepticism about its key provisions. Much of the Contract may fail to become law, not because of a Clinton veto, but because the Senate defeats the measures or fails to act on them.

Although the newly elected Republican senators are quite conservative, moderates retain far more power in the Senate than in the House. Senate Majority Leader Bob Dole is far more moderate than Gingrich, as are the chairs of many of the key committees. Dole is likely to seek the presidency in 1996, and will not want to spend his campaign defending the passage of unpopular legislation. Moreover, Dole and many other Senate Republicans are more concerned about the deficit than are House Republicans, and less willing to make very deep cuts in domestic spending.

The passage of the provisions in the Contract will ultimately depend on the ability of Gingrich and other House Republicans to negotiate with their counterparts in the Senate. Gingrich may find it difficult to win concessions from someone he once called "tax collector for the welfare state," and it is likely that many of the Contract's tax cuts will be moderated or eliminated by the more deficit-conscious Senate.

Democrats and Republicans in the 104th Congress

House Democrats find themselves in the unaccustomed position of minority party. As a majority party, Democrats ignored Republican proposals, locked them out of political negotiations, and governed with the confidence that their majority status would last forever. Although House Republicans spent much of the past decade imagining how they would govern when they finally won a majority, most Democrats had spent very little time before the election considering their strategies should they become a minority.

The elections changed the composition of the House Democrats, reducing by nearly half the number of moderate Democrats. The combined Black and Hispanic caucuses now constitute approximately a third of House Democrats, giving them an increased voice in policymaking, and presumably pulling the party to the left. The remaining southern and moderate Democrats interpret the 1994 elections to mean that the Democratic party should move toward the center, but such a move will be difficult in the 104th House. House Democrats will often find themselves unable to affect the legislative agenda of the Republicans, but the Republican majority is sufficiently narrow that a united Democratic party will be able to exert influence on at least some occasions.

Many House Republicans harbor some resentment toward the Democrats for the way they were excluded from policymaking. Soon after the election, ranking House Republicans began to recount incidents when they had approached a committee chair with a proposal, only to be told that their input was not wanted. A few Republicans have gleefully indicated that 1995 will be "payback time," but Gingrich and other party leaders have instead reached out to many House Democrats and promised to allow them to offer amendments and participate in a full debate of policy options.

The tone of this partisan interaction may be decided early in the term. On December 17, 1994, the Connecticut Supreme Court declared Democrat Sam Gejdenson the winner by twenty-one votes in the state's second House district. Republican candidate Edward W. Munster announced that he would appeal to the House of Representatives, which has the final say in certifying the outcome of elections. In 1985, the Democratic-controlled House in a party-line vote awarded a contested seat to Democrat Frank McCloskey in Indiana. Although the merits of the case are murky, Republicans believed that they were robbed, and staged a walkout in protest. If the Republican House certifies Munster in retaliation, a more partisan atmosphere is likely to prevail.

In the Senate, Democrats have the power to block passage of any bill, and are therefore in a position to negotiate the content of all major legislation. Many Senate Democrats served in the minority between 1980 and 1986, and understand the parliamentary strategies upon which the minority party relies. The composition of the Senate Democratic party was not changed markedly by the election: only two elected incumbents were defeated. Presumably the Senate Democrats will seek to forge coalitions with moderate Republicans to pass centrist legislation, and will filibuster other measures on which they are unable or unwilling to reach accord.

Wide World Photos

The Connecticut Citizens Action Group (CCAG) sponsored a petition calling for Congress to seat winning candidate Sam Gejdenson (D-Connecticut) in the House of Representatives. Gejdenson won Connecticut's race for House District 2 by a tiny margin over Republican Edward Munster, and it was feared that the Republican-controlled Congress would overturn this election.

CONCLUSION

The 1994 elections reversed a generation of Democratic dominance in the House, and presented Republicans with an unprecedented opportunity to mold policy at the national, state, and local levels. Although Democratic leaders, especially President Clinton, will be able to block legislation they oppose, they will be unable to advance a positive agenda without the cooperation of Republicans. Republicans will press their newfound gains with an ambitious program in the first 100 days of the new Congress.

Ultimately, neither Clinton nor the Republicans can govern effectively without the cooperation of the other. Clinton's negotiations with Republicans will be made more difficult by the united conservatism of Republicans in the House, and the greater liberalism of the surviving House Democrats. Negotiations may be easier in the Senate, where Democrats and Republicans have more cordial relations, and are less ideologically divided.

Whether the 1994 election was the "big one" that signals the solidification of a rolling realignment is not yet clear. Whatever the longevity of the Republican majority, however, it seems likely that the 1994 elections will reshape American politics and policy in the near future.

Critical
Thinking
Questions

1. What do we mean by a mandate? What would it take for an election to qualify as a mandate? Does the 1994 election qualify according to your criteria?

2. What do we mean by realignment? Do you think the Republicans have finally achieved a realignment? If so, is it national or regional? If not, why do you think there has not been a realignment?

3. How long do you predict the Republicans will control the House of Representatives? Think of three factors that point to long-term control and three that suggest Republican dominance will be short-lived.

4. Consider the changes that the Republicans have made to the structure and rules of the House. Which of these changes constitute improvements and which do not? What effect do you think they will have on how the House does its work?

5. Initially the Republicans proposed eliminating more committees, cutting the staff assigned to individual members, and reducing the congressional franking privilege, but they soon abandoned that effort. What sorts of institutional and personal considerations make these kinds of changes difficult? Do you think the Republican leadership should have backed away from its original proposals?

6. If you were an adviser to President Clinton, what strategies would you advise him to adopt in dealing with the new Congress? What issues should he emphasize? What policies should he accept, and where should he draw the line? How should he use his veto as a political weapon? Is your answer affected by whether Clinton is or is not a candidate for renomination and reelection?

7. If you were an adviser to Newt Gingrich, how would you advise him to proceed? Should he seek to compromise with Senate Republicans and the president? On which issues should he refuse to compromise?

Assume that Gingrich is motivated by the policy goals of the Republicans and by a desire to maintain and enlarge the Republican majority in the House.

8. If you were an adviser to Robert Dole, the Senate majority leader, how would you advise him to proceed? Should he and the Republicans offer their own agenda or accept the House's lead? Should Dole try to formulate his own policy proposals? Should he try to get the Senate to pass the Contract, or should he support and oppose various parts? Assume that Dole is motivated by policy goals and by a desire to be elected president in 1996.

9. Assess the strategies of the president and the House and Senate leadership since the elections. Who has been successful? Explain.

10. What are the principal lessons the candidates and parties should have learned from the 1994 elections? How can they apply these lessons to the politics of American government?

Additional Readings

Abramowitz, Alan I., and Jeffrey A. Segal. *Senate Elections.* Ann Arbor: University of Michigan Press, 1992.

Biersack, Robert, Paul S. Herrnson, and Clyde Wilcox. *Risky Business? PAC Decisionmaking in Congressional Elections.* New York: M. E. Sharpe, 1994.

Campbell, James E. *The Presidential Pulse of Congressional Elections.* Lexington, Ky.: University of Kentucky Press, 1993.

Cook, Elizabeth Adell, Sue Thomas, and Clyde Wilcox. *The Year of the Woman: Myths and Realities.* Boulder, Colo.: Westview Press, 1993.

Goldenberg, Edie N., and Michael W. Traugott. *Campaigning for Congress.* Washington, D.C.: Congressional Quarterly Press, 1984.

Herrnson, Paul S. *Congressional Elections: Campaigning at Home and in Washington.* Washington, D.C.: Congressional Quarterly Press, 1994.

Jacobson, Gary C. *The Politics of Congressional Elections.* 3rd ed. New York: HarperCollins, 1992.

Jacobson, Gary C., and Samuel Kernell. *Strategy and Choice in Congressional Elections.* New Haven: Yale University Press, 1982.

Kazee, Thomas A., ed. *Who Runs for Congress? Ambition, Context, and Candidate Emergence.* Washington, D.C.: Congressional Quarterly Press, 1994.

Lewis-Beck, Michael S., and Tom W. Rice. *Forecasting Elections.* Washington, D.C.: Congressional Quarterly Press, 1992.

Appendixes

Contract with America

As Republican Members of the House of Representatives and as citizens seeking to join that body we propose not just to change its policies, but even more important, to restore the bonds of trust between the people and their elected representatives.

That is why, in this era of official evasion and posturing, we offer instead a detailed agenda for national renewal, a written commitment with no fine print.

This year's election offers the chance, after four decades of one-party control, to bring to the House a new majority that will transform the way Congress works. That historic change would be the end of government that is too big, too intrusive, and too easy with the public's money. It can be the beginning of a Congress that respects the values and shares the faith of the American family.

Like Lincoln, our first Republican president, we intend to act "with firmness in the right, as God gives us to see the right." To restore accountability to Congress. To end its cycle of scandal and disgrace. To make us all proud again of the way free people govern themselves.

On the first day of the 104th Congress, the new Republican majority will immediately pass the following major reforms, aimed at restoring the faith and trust of the American people in their government:

FIRST, require all laws that apply to the rest of the country also apply equally to the Congress;

SECOND, select a major, independent auditing firm to conduct a comprehensive audit of Congress for waste, fraud or abuse;

THIRD, cut the number of House committees, and cut committee staff by one-third;

FOURTH, limit the terms of all committee chairs;

FIFTH, ban the casting of proxy votes in committee;

SIXTH, require committee meetings to be open to the public;

SEVENTH, require a three-fifths majority vote to pass a tax increase;

EIGHTH, guarantee an honest accounting of our Federal Budget by implementing zero base-line budgeting.

Thereafter, within the first 100 days of the 104th Congress, we shall bring to the House Floor the following bills, each to be given full and open debate, each to be given a clear and fair vote and each to be immediately available this day for public inspection and scrutiny.

1. THE FISCAL RESPONSIBILITY ACT

A balanced budget/tax limitation amendment and a legislative line-item veto to restore fiscal responsibility to an out-of-control Congress, requiring them to live under the same budget constraints as families and businesses.

2. THE TAKING BACK OUR STREETS ACT

An anti-crime package including stronger truth-in-sentencing, "good faith" exclusionary rule exemptions, effective death penalty provisions, and cuts in social spending from this summer's "crime" bill to fund prison construction and additional law enforcement to keep people secure in their neighborhoods and kids safe in their schools.

3. THE PERSONAL RESPONSIBILITY ACT

Discourage illegitimacy and teen pregnancy by prohibiting welfare to minor mothers and denying increased AFDC for additional children while on welfare, cut spending for welfare programs, and enact a tough two-years-and-out provision with work requirements to promote individual responsibility.

4. THE FAMILY REINFORCEMENT ACT

Child support enforcement, tax incentives for adoption, strengthening rights of parents in their children's education, stronger child pornography laws, and an elderly dependent care tax credit to reinforce the central role of families in American society.

5. THE AMERICAN DREAM RESTORATION ACT

A $500 per child tax credit, begin repeal of the marriage tax penalty, and creation of American Dream Savings Accounts to provide middle class tax relief.

6. THE NATIONAL SECURITY RESTORATION ACT

No U.S. troops under U.N. command and restoration of the essential parts of our national security funding to strengthen our national defense and maintain our credibility around the world.

7. THE SENIOR CITIZENS FAIRNESS ACT

Raise the Social Security earnings limit which currently forces seniors out of the work force, repeal the 1993 tax hikes on Social Security benefits and provide tax incentives for private long-term care insurance to let older Americans keep more of what they have earned over the years.

8. THE JOB CREATION AND WAGE ENHANCEMENT ACT

Small business incentives, capital gains cut [sic] and indexation, neutral cost recovery, risk assessment/cost-benefit analysis, strengthening the Regulatory Flexibility Act and unfunded mandate reform to create jobs and raise worker wages.

9. THE COMMON SENSE LEGAL REFORM ACT

"Loser pays" laws, reasonable limits on punitive damages and reform of product liability laws to stem the endless tide of litigation.

10. THE CITIZEN LEGISLATURE ACT

A first-ever vote on term limits to replace career politicians with citizen legislators.

Further, we will instruct the House Budget Committee to report to the floor and we will work to enact additional budget savings, beyond the budget cuts specifically included in the legislation described above, to ensure that the Federal budget deficit will be *less* than it would have been without the enactment of these bills.

Respecting the judgment of our fellow citizens as we seek their mandate for reform, we hereby pledge our names to this Contract with America.

_____   _____

Name   State/District

Governors

The names of governors elected in 1994 are marked with an * and incumbents appear in boldface.

Alabama—Rob James Jr. (R)*
Alaska—Tony Knowles (D)*
Arizona—Fife Symington (R)*
Arkansas—Jim Guy Tucker (D)*
California—Pete Wilson (R)*
Colorado—Roy Romer (D)*
Connecticut—John G. Rowland (R)*
Delaware—Thomas R. Carper (D)
Florida—Lawton Chiles (D)*
Georgia—Zell Miller (D)*
Hawaii—Benjamin J. Cayetano (D)*
Idaho—Phil Batt (R)*
Illinois—Jim Edgar (R)*
Indiana—Evan Bayh (D)
Iowa—Terry E. Branstad (R)*
Kansas—Bill Graves (R)*
Kentucky—Brereton Jones (D)
Louisiana—Edwin W. Edwards (D)
Maine—Angus King (I)*
Maryland—Parris Glendening (D)*
Massachusetts-William F. Weld (R)*
Michigan—John Engler (R)*
Minnesota—Arne Carlson (R)*
Mississippi—Kirk Fordice (R)
Missouri—Mel Carnahan (D)

Montana—Marc Racicot (R)
Nebraska—Ben Nelson (D)*
Nevada—Bob Miller (D)*
New Hampshire—Stephen Merrill (R)*
New Jersey—Christine Todd Whitman (R)
New Mexico—Gary E. Johnson (R)*
New York—George E. Pataki (R)*
North Carolina—James B. Hunt Jr. (D)
North Dakota—Edward T. Schafer (R)
Ohio—George V. Voinovich (R)*
Oklahoma—Frank Keating (R)*
Oregon—John Kitzhaber (D)*
Pennsylvania—Tom Ridge (R)*
Rhode Island—Lincoln C. Almond (R)*
South Carolina—David Beasley (R)*
South Dakota—William J. Janklow (R)*
Tennessee—Don Sundquist (R)*
Texas—George W. Bush (R)*
Utah—Michael O. Leavitt (R)
Vermont—Howard Dean (D)*
Virginia—George F. Allen (R)
Washington—Mike Lowry (D)
West Virginia—Gaston Caperton (D)
Wisconsin—Tommy G. Thompson (R)*
Wyoming—Jim Geringer (R)*

Senate Membership in the 104th Congress

Republicans 53
Democrats 47

1994 winners are marked with an * and seats that switched parties are in italics.

Alabama
Howell Heflin (D)
Richard C. Shelby (R)

Alaska
Ted Stevens (R)
Frank H. Murkowski (R)

Arizona
John McCain (R)
Jon Kyl (R) *

Arkansas
Dale Bumpers (D)
David Pryor (D)

California
Dianne Feinstein (D)*
Barbara Boxer (D)

Colorado
Hank Brown (R)
Ben Nighthorse Campbell (D)

Connecticut
Christopher J. Dodd (D)
Joseph I. Lieberman (D)*

Delaware
William V. Roth Jr. (R)*
Joseph R. Biden Jr. (D)

Florida
Bob Graham (D)
Connie Mack (R)*

Georgia
Sam Nunn (D)
Paul Coverdell (R)

Hawaii
Daniel K. Inouye (D)
Daniel K. Akaka (D)*

Idaho
Larry E. Craig (R)
Dirk Kempthorne (R)

Illinois
Paul Simon (D)
Carol Moseley-Braun (D)

Indiana
Richard G. Lugar (R)*
Daniel R. Coats (R)

Iowa
Charles E. Grassley (R)
Tom Harkin (D)

Kansas
Bob Dole (R)
Nancy Landon Kassebaum (R)

Kentucky
Wendell H. Ford (D)
Mitch McConnell (R)

Louisiana
J. Bennett Johnston (D)
John B. Breaux (D)

Maine
William S. Cohen (R)
Olympia J. Snowe (R) *

Maryland
Paul S. Sarbanes (D)
Barbara A. Mikulski (D)

Massachusetts
Edward M. Kennedy (D)*
John Kerry (D)

Michigan
Carl Levin (D)
*Spencer Abraham (R)**

Minnesota
Paul Wellstone (D)
Rod Grams (R)*

Mississippi
Thad Cochran (R)
Trent Lott (R)*

Missouri
Christopher S. Bond (R)
John Ashcroft (R)*

Montana
Max Baucus (D)
Conrad Burns (R)*

Nebraska
Jim Exon (D)
Bob Kerrey (D)*

Nevada
Harry Reid (D)
Richard H. Bryan (D)*

New Hampshire
Robert C. Smith (R)
Judd Gregg (R)

New Jersey
Bill Bradley (D)
Frank R. Lautenberg (D)*

New Mexico
Pete V. Domenici (R)
Jeff Bingaman (D)*

New York
Daniel Patrick Moynihan (D)*
Alfonse M. D'Amato (R)

North Carolina
Jesse Helms (R)
Lauch Faircloth (R)

North Dakota
Kent Conrad (D)*
Byron L. Dorgan (D)

Ohio
John Glenn (D)
*Mike DeWine (R)**

Oklahoma
Don Nickles (R)
*James M. Inhofe (R)**

Oregon
Mark O. Hatfield (R)
Bob Packwood (R)

Pennsylvania
Arlen Specter (R)
*Rick Santorum (R)**

Rhode Island
Claiborne Pell (D)
John H. Chafee (R)*

South Carolina
Strom Thurmond (R)
Ernest F. Hollings (D)

South Dakota
Larry Pressler (R)
Tom Daschle (D)

Tennessee
*Fred Thompson (R)**
*Bill Frist (R)**

Texas
Phil Gramm (R)
Kay Bailey Hutchison (R)*

Utah
Orrin G. Hatch (R)*
Robert F. Bennett (R)

Vermont
Patrick J. Leahy (D)
James M. Jeffords (R)*

Virginia
John W. Warner (R)
Charles S. Robb (D)*

Washington
Slade Gorton (R)*
Patty Murray (D)

West Virginia
Robert C. Byrd (D)*
John D. Rockefeller IV (D)

Wisconsin
Herb Kohl (D)*
Russell D. Feingold (D)

Wyoming
Alan K. Simpson (R)
Craig Thomas (R)*

House Membership in the 104th Congress

Republicans 230   Freshmen 73
Democrats 204   Freshmen 13
Independent 1

*Freshman representative

Alabama
1 Sonny Callahan (R)
2 Terry Everett (R)
3 Glen Browder (D)
4 Tom Bevill (D)
5 Robert E. "Bud" Cramer (D)
6 Spencer Bachus (R)
7 Earl F. Hilliard (D)

Alaska
AL Don Young (R)

Arizona
1 Matt Salmon (R)*
2 Ed Pastor (D)
3 Bob Stump (R)
4 John Shadegg (R)*
5 Jim Kolbe (R)
6 J. D. Hayworth (R)*

Arkansas
1 Blanche Lambert (D)
2 Ray Thornton (D)
3 Tim Hutchinson (R)
4 Jay Dickey (R)

California
1 Frank Riggs (R)*
2 Wally Herger (R)
3 Vic Fazio (D)
4 John T. Doolittle (R)
5 Robert T. Matsui (D)
6 Lynn Woolsey (D)
7 George Miller (D)
8 Nancy Pelosi (D)
9 Ronald V. Dellums (D)
10 Bill Baker (R)
11 Richard W. Pombo (R)
12 Tom Lantos (D)
13 Pete Stark (D)
14 Anna G. Eshoo (D)
15 Norman Y. Mineta (D)
16 Zoe Lofgren (D)*
17 Sam Farr (D)
18 Gary A. Condit (D)
19 George P. Radanovich (R)*
20 Cal Dooley (D)
21 Bill Thomas (R)
22 Andrea Seastrand (R)*
23 Elton Gallegly (R)
24 Anthony C. Beilenson (D)
25 Howard P. "Buck" McKeon (R)
26 Howard L. Berman (D)
27 Carlos J. Moorhead (R)
28 David Dreier (R)
29 Henry A. Waxman (D)
30 Xavier Becerra (D)
31 Matthew G. Martinez (D)
32 Julian C. Dixon (D)
33 Lucille Roybal-Allard (D)
34 Esteban E. Torres (D)

35 Maxine Walters (D)
36 Jane Harmon (D)
37 Walter R. Tucker III (D)
38 Steve Horn (R)
39 Ed Royce (R)
40 Jerry Lewis (R)
41 Jay C. Kim (R)
42 George E. Brown Jr. (D)
43 Ken Calvert (R)
44 Sonny Bono (R)*
45 Dana Rohrabacher (R)
46 Robert K. Dornan (R)
47 Christopher Cox (R)
48 Ron Packard (R)
49 Brian P. Bilbray (R)*
50 Bob Filner (D)
51 Randy "Duke" Cunningham (R)
52 Duncan Hunter (R)

Colorado
 1 Patricia Schroeder (D)
 2 David E. Skaggs (D)
 3 Scott McInnis (R)
 4 Wayne Allard (R)
 5 Joel Hefley (R)
 6 Dan Schaefer (R)

Connecticut
 1 Barbara B. Kennelly (D)
 2 Sam Gejdenson (D)
 3 Rosa DeLauro (D)
 4 Christopher Shays (R)
 5 Gary A. Franks (R)
 6 Nancy L. Johnson (R)

Delaware
AL Michael N. Castle (R)

Florida
 1 Joe Scarborough (R)*
 2 Pete Peterson (D)
 3 Corrine Brown (D)
 4 Tillie Fowler (R)
 5 Karen L. Thurman (D)
 6 Cliff Stearns (R)
 7 John L. Mica (R)
 8 Bill McCollum (R)
 9 Michael Bilirakis (R)
10 C.W. "Bill" Young (R)
11 Sam M. Gibbons (D)
12 Charles T. Canady (R)

13 Dan Miller (R)
14 Porter J. Goss (R)
15 Dave Weldon (R)*
16 Mark Foley (R)*
17 Carrie P. Meek (D)
18 Ileana Ros-Lehtinen (R)
19 Harry A. Johnston (D)
20 Peter Deutsch (D)
21 Lincoln Diaz-Balart (R)
22 E. Clay Shaw Jr. (R)
23 Alcee L. Hastings (D)

Georgia
 1 Jack Kingston (R)
 2 Sanford D. Bishop Jr. (D)
 3 Mac Collins (R)
 4 John Linder (R)
 5 John Lewis (D)
 6 Newt Gingrich (R)
 7 Bob Barr (R)*
 8 Saxby Chambliss (R)*
 9 Nathan Deal (D)
10 Charlie Norwood (R)*
11 Cynthia A. McKinney (D)

Hawaii
 1 Neil Abercrombie (D)
 2 Patsy T. Mink (D)

Idaho
 1 Helen Chenoweth (R)*
 2 Michael D. Crapo (R)

Illinois
 1 Bobby L. Rush (D)
 2 Mel Reynolds (D)
 3 William O. Lipinski (D)
 4 Luis V. Gutierrez (D)
 5 Michael Patrick Flanagan (R)*
 6 Henry J. Hyde (R)
 7 Cardiss Collins (D)
 8 Philip M. Crane (R)
 9 Sidney R. Yates (D)
10 John Edward Porter (R)
11 Gerald C. "Jerry" Weller (R)*
12 Jerry F. Costello (D)
13 Harris W. Fawell (R)
14 Dennis Hastert (R)
15 Thomas W. Ewing (R)
16 Donald Manzullo (R)
17 Lane Evans (D)
18 Ray LaHood (R)*

19 Glenn Poshard (D)
20 Richard J. Durbin (D)

Indiana
  1 Peter J. Visclosky (D)
  2 David M. McIntosh (R)*
  3 Tim Roemer (D)
  4 Mark Edward Souder (R)*
  5 Steve Buyer (R)
  6 Dan Burton (R)
  7 John T. Myers (R)
  8 John Hostettler (R)*
  9 Lee H. Hamilton (D)
 10 Andrew Jacobs Jr. (D)

Iowa
  1 Jim Leach (R)
  2 Jim Nussle (R)
  3 Jim Ross Lightfoot (R)
  4 Greg Ganske (R)*
  5 Tom Latham (R)*

Kansas
  1 Pat Roberts (R)
  2 Sam Brownback (R)*
  3 Jan Meyers (R)
  4 Todd Tiahrt (R)*

Kentucky
  1 Edward Whitfield (R)*
  2 Ron Lewis (R)
  3 Mike Ward (D)*
  4 Jim Bunning (R)
  5 Harold Rogers (R)
  6 Scotty Baesler (D)

Louisiana
  1 Robert L. Livingston (R)
  2 William J. Jefferson (D)
  3 W. J. "Billy" Tauzin (D)
  4 Cleo Fields (D)
  5 Jim McCrery (R)
  6 Richard H. Baker (R)
  7 Jimmy Hayes (D)

Maine
  1 James B. Longley Jr. (R)*
  2 John Baldacci (D)*

Maryland
  1 Wayne T. Gilchrest (R)
  2 Robert L. Ehrlich Jr. (R)*
  3 Benjamin L. Cardin (D)

  4 Albert R. Wynn (D)
  5 Steny H. Hoyer (D)
  6 Roscoe G. Bartlett (R)
  7 Kweisi Mfume (D)
  8 Constance A. Morella (R)

Massachusetts
  1 John W. Olver (D)
  2 Richard E. Neal (D)
  3 Peter I. Blute (R)
  4 Barney Frank (D)
  5 Martin T. Meehan (D)
  6 Peter G. Torkildsen (R)
  7 Edward J. Markey (D)
  8 Joseph P. Kennedy II (D)
  9 Joe Moakley (D)
 10 Gerry E. Studds (D)

Michigan
  1 Bart Stupak (D)
  2 Peter Hoekstra (R)
  3 Vernon J. Ehlers (R)
  4 Dave Camp (R)
  5 James A. Barcia (D)
  6 Fred Upton (R)
  7 Nick Smith (R)
  8 Dick Chrysler (R)*
  9 Dale E. Kildee (D)
 10 David E. Bonior (D)
 11 Joe Knollenberg (R)
 12 Sander M. Levin (D)
 13 Lynn Nancy Rivers (D)*
 14 John Conyers Jr. (D)
 15 Barbara-Rose Collins (D)
 16 John D. Dingell (D)

Minnesota
  1 Gil Gutknecht (R)*
  2 David Minge (D)
  3 Jim Ramstad (R)
  4 Bruce F. Vento (D)
  5 Martin Olav Sabo (D)
  6 William P. "Bill" Luther (D)*
  7 Collin C. Peterson (D)
  8 James L. Oberstar (D)

Mississippi
  1 Roger Wicker (R)*
  2 Bennie Thompson (D)
  3 G.V. "Sonny" Montgomery (D)
  4 Mike Parker (D)
  5 Gene Taylor (D)

Missouri
1 William L. Clay (D)
2 James M. Talent (R)
3 Richard A. Gephardt (D)
4 Ike Skelton (D)
5 Karen McCarthy (D)*
6 Pat Danner (D)
7 Mel Hancock (R)
8 Bill Emerson (R)
9 Harold L. Volkmer (D)

Montana
AL Pat Williams (D)

Nebraska
1 Doug Bereuter (R)
2 Jon Christensen (R)*
3 Bill Barrett (R)

Nevada
1 John Ensign (R)*
2 Barbara F. Vucanovich (R)

New Hampshire
1 Bill Zeliff (R)
2 Charles Bass (R)*

New Jersey
1 Robert E. Andrews (D)
2 Frank A. LoBiondo (R)*
3 H. James Saxton (R)
4 Christopher H. Smith (R)
5 Marge Roukema (R)
6 Frank Pallone Jr. (D)
7 Bob Franks (R)
8 Bill Martini (R)*
9 Robert G. Torricelli (D)
10 Donald M. Payne (D)
11 Rodney Frelinghuysen (R)*
12 Dick Zimmer (R)
13 Robert Menendez (D)

New Mexico
1 Steven H. Schiff (R)
2 Joe Skeen (R)
3 Bill Richardson (D)

New York
1 Michael P. Forbes (R)*
2 Rick A. Lazio (R)
3 Peter T. King (R)
4 Daniel Frisa (R)*
5 Gary L. Ackerman (D)
6 Floyd H. Flake (D)

7 Thomas J. Manton (D)
8 Jerrold Nadler (D)
9 Charles E. Schumer (D)
10 Edolphus Towns (D)
11 Major R. Owens (D)
12 Nydia M. Velázquez (D)
13 Susan Molinari (R)
14 Carolyn B. Maloney (D)
15 Charles B. Rangel (D)
16 Jose E. Serrano (D)
17 Eliot L. Engel (D)
18 Nita M. Lowey (D)
19 Sue W. Kelly (R)*
20 Benjamin A. Gilman (R)
21 Michael R. McNulty (D)
22 Gerald B. H. Solomon (R)
23 Sherwood Boehlert (R)
24 John M. McHugh (R)
25 James T. Walsh (R)
26 Maurice D. Hinchey (D)
27 Bill Paxon (R)
28 Louise M. Slaughter (D)
29 John J. LaFalce (D)
30 Jack Quinn (R)
31 Amo Houghton (R)

North Carolina
1 Eva Clayton (D)
2 David Funderburk (R)*
3 Walter B. Jones Jr. (R)*
4 Frederick Kenneth Heineman (R)*
5 Richard M. Burr (R)*
6 Howard Coble (R)
7 Charlie Rose (D)
8 W. G. "Bill" Hefner (D)
9 Sue Myrick (R)*
10 Cass Ballenger (R)
11 Charles H. Taylor (R)
12 Melvin Watt (D)

North Dakota
AL Earl Pomeroy (D)

Ohio
1 Steve Chabot (R)*
2 Rob Portman (R)
3 Tony P. Hall (D)
4 Michael G. Oxley (R)
5 Paul E. Gillmor (R)
6 Frank A. Cremeans (R)*
7 David L. Hobson (R)

8 John A. Boehner (R)
9 Marcy Kaptur (D)
10 Martin R. Hoke (R)
11 Louis Stokes (D)
12 John R. Kasich (R)
13 Sherrod Brown (D)
14 Tom Sawyer (D)
15 Deborah Pryce (R)
16 Ralph Regula (R)
17 James A. Traficant Jr. (D)
18 Bob Ney (R)*
19 Steven C. LaTourette (R)*

Oklahoma
1 Steve Largent (R)*
2 Tom Coburn (R)*
3 Bill Brewster (D)
4 J. C. Watts (R)*
5 Ernest Jim Istook Jr. (R)
6 Frank D. Lucas (R)

Oregon
1 Elizabeth Furse (D)
2 Wes Cooley (R)*
3 Ron Wyden (D)
4 Peter A. DeFazio (D)
5 Jim Bunn (R)*

Pennsylvania
1 Thomas A. Fogiletta (D)
2 Chaka Fattah (D)*
3 Robert A. Borski (D)
4 Ron Klink (D)
5 William F. Clinger (R)
6 Tim Holden (D)
7 Curt Weldon (R)
8 James C. Greenwood (R)
9 Bud Shuster (R)
10 Joseph M. McDade (R)
11 Paul E. Kanjorski (D)
12 John P. Murtha (D)
13 Jon D. Fox (R)*
14 William J. Coyne (D)
15 Paul McHale (D)
16 Robert S. Walker (R)
17 George W. Gekas (R)
18 Mike Doyle (D)*
19 Bill Goodling (R)
20 Frank R. Mascara (D)*
21 Phil English (R)*

Rhode Island
1 Patrick J. Kennedy (D)*
2 Jack Reed (D)

South Carolina
1 Marshall "Mark" Sanford (R)*
2 Floyd D. Spence (R)
3 Lindsey Graham (R)*
4 Bob Inglis (R)
5 John M. Spratt Jr. (D)
6 James E. Clyburn (D)

South Dakota
AL Tim Johnson (D)

Tennessee
1 James H. Quillen (R)
2 John J. "Jimmy" Duncan Jr. (R)
3 Zach Wamp (R)*
4 Van Hilleary (R)*
5 Bob Clement (D)
6 Bart Gordon (D)
7 Ed Bryant (R)*
8 John Tanner (D)
9 Harold E. Ford (D)

Texas
1 Jim Chapman (D)
2 Charles Wilson (D)
3 Sam Johnson (R)
4 Ralph M. Hall (D)
5 John Bryant (D)
6 Joe L. Barton (R)
7 Bill Archer (R)
8 Jack Fields (R)
9 Steve Stockman (R)*
10 Lloyd Doggett (D)*
11 Chet Edwards (D)
12 Pete Geren (D)
13 William M. "Mac" Thornberry (R)*
14 Greg Laughlin (D)
15 E. "Kika" de la Garza (D)
16 Ronald D. Coleman (D)
17 Charles W. Stenholm (D)
18 Sheila Jackson Lee (D)*
19 Larry Combest (R)
20 Henry B. Gonzalez (D)
21 Lamar Smith (R)
22 Tom DeLay (R)
23 Henry Bonilla (R)
24 Martin Frost (D)

25 Ken Bentsen (D)*
26 Dick Armey (R)
27 Solomon P. Ortiz (D)
28 Frank Tejeda (D)
29 Gene Green (D)
30 Edie Bernice Johnson (D)

Utah
1 James V. Hansen (R)
2 Enid Greene Waldholtz (R)*
3 Bill Orton (D)

Vermont
AL Bernard Sanders (I)

Virginia
1 Herbert H. Bateman (R)
2 Owen B. Pickett (D)
3 Robert C. Scott (D)
4 Norman Sisisky (D)
5 L. F. Payne Jr. (D)
6 Robert W. Goodlatte (R)
7 Thomas J. Bliley Jr. (R)
8 James P. Moran (D)
9 Rick Boucher (D)
10 Frank R. Wolf (R)
11 Thomas M. Davis III (R)*

Washington
1 Rick White (R)*
2 Jack Metcalf (R)*
3 Linda Smith (R)*
4 Doc Hastings (R)*
5 George Nethercutt (R)*
6 Norm Dicks (D)
7 Jim McDermott (D)
8 Jennifer Dunn (R)
9 Randy Tate (R)*

West Virginia
1 Alan B. Mollohan (D)
2 Bob Wise (D)
3 Nick J. Rahall II (D)

Wisconsin
1 Mark W. Neumann (R)*
2 Scott L. Klug (R)
3 Steve Gunderson (R)
4 Gerald D. Kleczka (D)
5 Thomas M. Barrett (D)
6 Tom Petri (R)
7 David R. Obey (D)
8 Toby Roth (R)
9 F. James Sensenbrenner Jr. (R)

Wyoming
AL Barbara Cubin (R)*

Notes

1. James E. Campbell, "Reading the GOP's Tea Leaves," *Washington Times*, Nov. 6, 1994, B5.
2. Michael S. Lewis-Beck and Tom W. Rice, *Forecasting Elections* (Washington, D.C.: Congressional Quarterly Press, 1992).
3. John M. Berry, "Economy Shows Solid 3.4% Gain," *Washington Post*, Oct. 29, 1994, A1. A CBS News pre-election poll showed that a majority of voters thought the economy was still in recession and that most who thought the economy was doing well did not credit Clinton.
4. Gary C. Jacobson and Samuel Kernell, *Strategy and Choice in Congressional Elections* (New Haven: Yale University Press, 1981).
5. The Democratic pool was less impressive than Jacobson's model would have predicted, suggesting that potential Democratic candidates looked at the poll results and decided to sit out this election.
6. Personal communication.
7. Personal communication.
8. James E. Campbell notes that if Perot voters are treated as anti-Republican voters, then the estimate of the Democratic "surge" is greater, and the consequent predicted "decline" is also greater.
9. *Akron Beacon Journal*, Nov. 9, 1994, 1.
10. Exit polls have asked different versions of the born-again item over the years, making the value of comparisons tenuous.
11. The distinction here is an important one. Some white born-again Christians are members of the Christian Right. Some are neutral toward organizations such as the Christian Coalition, and some oppose them. A few are even members of organizations such as People for the American Way, which is organized primarily to oppose the Christian Right.
12. Personal communication.
13. Cited in *Hotline Weekly Report*, Nov. 14, 1994, 12.
14. *Washington Post*, Nov. 26, 1994, A5.
15. Personal communication.
16. Quoted in *USA Today*, Nov. 11, 1994.

17. See Robert Dahl, "The Myth of the Presidential Mandate," in Stephen J. Wayne and Clyde Wilcox, *Quest for National Office* (New York: St. Martin's Press, 1992), pp. 265-275.

18. Those who guessed had a 50 percent chance of getting the right answer, since there are only two major parties. It is safe to assume that the 12 percent who guessed Republicans were matched by an equal 12 percent who luckily guessed Democrats.

19. Data from the 1990 National Election Study, again corrected for guessing.

20. The one referendum that failed was a measure in Utah, which had earlier passed term limits. The 1994 referendum sought to reduce the number of terms allowed. A similar measure passed in Colorado.

21. Interestingly, fully 6 percent of those who cast votes to oppose Clinton voted for Democratic candidates, while 6 percent of those who indicated that their vote was in support of Clinton voted for a Republican for the House.

22. Republican recruiters have had a difficult time convincing potential candidates to seek election to a legislative body in which they would be effectively denied a role in policy formulation.

23. Juan Williams, "Blacked Out in the New Congress," *Washington Post*, Nov. 20, 1994, C1.

24. *Washington Post*, Nov. 10, 1994, A1.

25. These figures overstate the differences somewhat, for Flanagan was the beneficiary of substantial coordinated spending by Republican party committees, and Rostenkowski spent a substantial percentage of his total during his primary election contest.

26. See Robert Biersack, Paul S. Herrnson, and Clyde Wilcox, *Risky Business: PAC Decisionmaking in Congressional Elections* (New York: M. E. Sharpe, 1994).

27. Cited in Robin Toner, "Bitter Tone of the '94 Campaign Elicits Worry on Public Debate," *New York Times*, Nov. 13, 1994, A1.

28. Reprinted in *New York Times,* Nov. 13, 1994, 20.

29. Personal communication. Williams also notes that not all advertising was bitterly negative. He cites an ad by Jim Jonz in his losing race against Senator Lugar of Indiana, in which Jonz visited towns in the state like Peru, Lebanon, and Mexico, looking for the foreign-aid dollars that Lugar had supported, or Ben Jones's MTV-style hip-hop song, "Newt . . . NOT!"

30. Cited in *Hotline Weekly Report*, Oct. 17, 1994.

31. Guy Gugliotta, "New Priorities Reflected by GOP Nomenclature," *Washington Post,* Dec. 3, 1994, A4.

32. Cited in *Congressional Quarterly Weekly Report,* Nov. 12, 1994, 3221.

33. Cited in *Congressional Quarterly Weekly Report,* Nov. 19, 1994, 3320.

34. Ibid.

35. Cited in *Congressional Quarterly Weekly Report,* Nov. 19, 1994, 3321.

36. Cited in *Washington Post,* Dec. 18, 1994, A29.

37. NPR interview, Nov. 1994.

38. Kevin Merida, "Republicans' Showing in Elections Renews Gay Rights Debate," *Washington Post,* Nov. 25, 1994, A33.

39. One obvious risk is to inspire an election-debate sound bite in which a Republican claims, "I knew Harry Truman. Harry Truman was a friend of mine. And, Mr. President, you're no Harry Truman."

Index

Throughout this index, the lowercase letters *c, m,* and *t* refer to captions, maps, and tables respectively.